Corgi Modern Poets in Focus: 2

Edited by
JEREMY ROBSON

CORGI BOOKS
TRANSWORLD PUBLISHERS LTD
A National General Company

CORGI MODERN POETS IN FOCUS: 2

A CORGI BOOK 0 552 08787 4

First publication in Great Britain

PRINTING HISTORY

Corgi edition published 1971

Introductions and selection © Jeremy Robson, 1971

Acknowledgements for the use of copyright material
will be found on page 8 which is hereby made part
of this copyright page.

Corgi Books are published by Transworld
Publishers Ltd.,
Cavendish House, 57-59 Uxbridge Road,
Ealing, London W.5.
Made and printed in Great Britain by
Cox & Wyman Ltd., London, Reading and Fakenham

Contents

ACKNOWLEDGEMENTS

For poems by Philip Larkin, to the author for 'The Cardplayers', 'Sad Steps', 'To the Sea'; to the Marvel Press for 'Reasons for Attendance', 'Church Going', 'At Grass' from *The Less Deceived* (1955); to Faber & Faber for 'Broadcast', 'Reference Back', 'Love Songs in Age', from *The Whitsun Weddings* (1964). For poems by Thomas Blackburn, to the author for 'Hospital for Defectives', 'A Point of Honour', 'En Route', 'A Small Keen Wind', 'Teaching Wordsworth', 'Schiara' from *A Breathing Space* (1964); to Putnam & Company for 'A Smell of Burning', 'Pasiphaë', 'For a Child' from *A Smell of Burning* (1961); to MacGibbon & Kee for 'Broken Image', 'Laudanum', 'All the Immortals' from *The Fourth Man* (1971). For poems by Keith Douglas to Faber & Faber for poems from *Selected Poems: Keith Douglas* (1964). For poems by Seamus Heaney, to the author for 'Shore Woman' and 'Limbo'; to Faber & Faber for 'Follower' from *Death of a Naturalist* (1966) and 'The Outlaw', 'Thatcher', 'Requiem for the Croppies', 'The Wife's Tale', 'The Forge', 'Elegy for a Still-Born Child', 'The Given Note' from *Door into the Dark* (1969). For poems by William Meredith, to the author for 'Grievances', to the author and *The Saturday Review* for 'A Mild Spoken Citizen'; to Alfred A. Knopf, Inc. for poems from *Earth Walk: New and Selected Poems* (1970). The excerpt by Philip Larkin from the Poetry Book Society Bulletin (1964) is published by permission of the Arts Council; the interview with Thomas Blackburn from *The Poet Speaks* (Routledge, 1966) by permission of the author; 'The Necessity of Poetry' by William Meredith (© *The Christian Science Monitor*) by permission of the author: the poem 'Do Not Embrace Your Mind's New Negro Friend' by William Meredith (© Princeton University Press, 1948) by permission of the author.

CORGI MODERN POETS IN FOCUS: 2

WILFRED OWEN

WILFRED OWEN was born at Oswestry in Shropshire in March 1893, and educated at the Birkenhead Institute and London University. Twenty-five years later he was dead, killed by machine-gun fire while encouraging his company across the Sambre Canal in France. For many critics he is the outstanding poet of the First World War, though some would reserve that accolade for Isaac Rosenberg or Siegfried Sassoon. In his Introduction to Owen's *Collected Poems* C. Day Lewis went so far as to call Owen's war poems 'the finest written by any poet of the First World War and probably the greatest about war in our literature'.

Yet Owen's reputation rests on only a small number of poems, his earliest work being heavily influenced by Keats, whose melancholy shadow falls heavily across so much of his writing. As Day Lewis remarked, 'Owen had not merely fallen in love with Keats; he felt for him at once a reverence and a strong affinity'. But Owen's influences were not purely English. In 1913, following a severe illness, he went to Bordeaux to escape the English winter. He took a job there as a tutor and was fortunate to meet the French poet Laurent Tailhade, who introduced him to contemporary French poetry. Thus, as another poet of that war, Edmund Blunden, has written, 'Owen had the advantage of being attuned to the sadness of the French poets'. 'At times,' Blunden added, 'he was the English Verlaine.'

At this stage Owen was still unsure of his own direction, and his attitude to poetry strangely casual. 'I certainly believe,' he wrote in 1914, 'I could make a better musician than many who profess to be, and are accepted as such. Mark, I do not for a moment call myself a musician, nor do I suspect I ever shall be, but there! I love Music, with such *strength* that I have had to conceal the passion, for fear it be thought weakness. . . . Failing Music, is it Pictures that I hanker to do? I am not ashamed to admit it, but heigh ho! . . . Let me now seriously and shamelessly work out a Poem.'

There is something of the dilettante about this, and in the prose style an echo of the flippant 90's. There is none of the concern for the craft of poetry, or its future, none of the commitment and fervour which he was later to show and which many of his contemporaries were displaying – D. H. Lawrence, for instance, who proclaimed in a letter: 'The essence of poetry with us in this age of stark and unlovely actualities is a stark directness, without a shadow of a lie or a deflection anywhere. Everything can go, but this stark, bare, rocky directness of statement, this alone makes poetry today.'

In 1915 Owen returned from France and enlisted. In June 1916 he was commissioned into the Manchester Regiment which, in January of the following year, was transferred to the Somme battlefield. He wrote to his brother: 'There is a fine heroic feeling about being in France, and I am in perfect spirits. A tinge of excitement is about me.' Two weeks later the tone had changed, as dramatically as the tone of his poetry was to change: 'I can see no excuse for deceiving you about these last 4 days. I have suffered seventh hell. I have not been at the front. I have been in front of it. I held an advanced post, that is, a "dug-out" in the middle of No Man's Land. We had a march of 3 miles over shelled road, then nearly 3 along a flooded trench. After that we came to where the trenches had been blown flat out and had to go over the top. It was of course dark, too dark, and the ground was not mud, not sloppy mud, but an octopus of sucking clay, 3, 4, and 5 feet deep, relieved only by craters full of water. Men have been known to drown in them. Many stuck in the mud. . . .'

Gradually the war, which had seemed to Owen distant and abstract, flooded his consciousness, and before long his poetry. D. J. Enright has expressed the view that although Owen's subject was war, 'war did not *make* him a poet, and peace, what we call peace, would not have unmade him'. Nevertheless the change in Owen's work from romanticism to realism, from abstraction to actuality, was rapid. Gone are the capital L's for Life and Love, and lines like; 'Birds/Cheerily chirping in the early day. /Bards/Singing of summer scything thro' the hay. . . .' Suddenly the tone is solemn, flat, direct, the imagery exact and compelling:

> Our brains ache, in the merciless iced east winds
>   that knive us . . .
> Wearied we keep awake because the night is silent . . .
> Low, drooping flares confuse our memory of the salient . . .
> Worried by silence, sentries whisper, curious, nervous,
>   But nothing happens.
>
> Watching, we hear the mad gusts tugging on the wire,
> Like twitching agonies of men among its brambles.
> Northward, incessantly, the flickering gunnery rumbles . . .

Here too are the half-rhymes, and the sombre orchestrations for which Owen is noted – the sounds and the hints of sounds which Benjamin Britten so accurately reflected in setting Owen's poems for his *War Requiem*. There are too in these lines unexpected associations and correlations: the wind, the wire, and the twitching men; the silence preventing sleep, making the sentries nervous.

*   *   *

After five months in the trenches, Owen was invalided home, his nerves shattered. At Craiglockhart War Hospital in

Edinburgh, where he was sent to recover, he met Captain Siegfried Sassoon, whose work he admired. Owen has described his meeting with the elder poet: 'Sassoon called me in to him; and having condemned some of my poems, amended others, and rejoiced over a few, he read me his very last works, which are superb beyond anything in his book. . . . I don't tell him so, or that I am not worthy to light his pipe.' Of their meeting and subsequent friendship, Edmund Blunden has written: 'To ascribe to it altogether the subsequent self-revelation of Owen as a poet would be incorrect, but the impact of Mr. Sassoon's character, thought, and independent poetic method gave the other a new purpose.' Apart from encouraging Owen personally, Sassoon introduced him to other poets, including Robert Graves and Robert Nichols, who were impressed with his talent: 'I have found a new poet for you,' Graves wrote to his friend Edward Marsh, 'just discovered, one Wilfred Owen: this is a real find, not a sudden lo here! or lo there! . . . but the real thing, when we've educated him a trifle more. R.N. and S.S. and myself are doing it!'

Owen returned to his old battalion on the front, as Company Commander. In the course of just a few months he evolved into a poet of stature, his work full of compassion for the men around him, of pity for their plight, of anger at those responsible for it:

> What passing-bells for these who die as cattle?
> Only the monstrous anger of the guns.
> Only the stuttering rifles' rapid rattle
> Can patter out their hasty orisons.

'All a poet can do today is warn,' wrote Owen in the Preface he was drafting for a planned book of poems. Yet he did more than that; for by focusing on the particulars of war and on the men involved in it, he caught something not only of

14

war's horrors, but of the dignity of man himself. Also, because he managed under hellish conditions to order his poetry, to fashion it, he created an elegy that was relevant both to those who died in that war, and for men caught in war's cross-fire everywhere. In the poetry itself, the eye is on detail – something that W. B. Yeats found unpalatable ('He is all blood, dirt, and sucked sugar-sticks'). Certainly the poems spill on occasions into melodrama, and from the cancellations and changes in the drafts of his poems one can see that Owen was aware of this. But in the best poems the tendency is mastered:

> If in some smothering dreams you too could pace
> Behind the wagon that we flung him in,
> And watch the white eyes writhing in his face,
> His hanging face, like a devil's sick of sin;

Everything is in close-up. The stare is hard, unflinching. The eyes are unforgettable, as is the dark music and the sardonic snarl with which the poem ('Dulce et Decorum Est') ends. Much has been made of Owen's technical achievement, and his telling use of half-rhyme and assonance. But it is the way he used them, rather than the devices themselves (which were by no means new to poetry), which is important: the way they have been made organic to the poem itself, so that they are there, as part of the structure, are carried and covered by the flow of the poetry itself and do not intrude:

> Courage was mine, and I had mystery,
> Wisdom was mine, and I had mastery:

In his study of Owen's work, D. S. R. Welland says of these assonant endings: 'You cannot imagine them used for any other purpose save Owen's, or by any other hand save his. They are the very modulation of his voice.'

In October 1918 Owen was awarded the Military Cross for exceptional bravery in the field; in November he was killed. Whether or not it was the war which made Owen a poet seems hardly relevant. What one can say is that in it he found his subject matter, and through it his voice.

Wilfred Owen writes: *

This book is not about heroes. English poetry is not yet fit to speak of them.

Nor is it about deeds, or lands, nor anything about glory, honour, might, majesty, dominion, or power, except War.

Above all I am not concerned with Poetry.

My subject is War, and the pity of War.

The Poetry is in the pity.

Yet these elegies are to this generation in no sense consolatory. They may be to the next. All a poet can do today is warn. That is why the true Poets must be truthful.

(If I thought the letter of this book would last, I might have used proper names; but if the spirit of it survives – survives Prussia – my ambition and those names will have achieved themselves fresher fields than Flanders. . . .)

---

* This Preface for a planned book of poems was found among Owen's papers after his death.

SHADWELL STAIR

I am the ghost of Shadwell Stair.
   Along the wharves by the water-house,
   And through the dripping slaughter-house,
I am the shadow that walks there.

  Yet I have flesh both firm and cool,
   And eyes tumultuous as the gems
   Of moons and lamps in the lapping Thames
When dusk sails wavering down the pool.

Shuddering the purple street-arc burns
   Where I watch always; from the banks
   Dolorously the shipping clanks,
And after me a strange tide turns.

I walk till the stars of London wane
   And dawn creeps up the Shadwell Stair.
   But when the crowing syrens blare
I with another ghost am lain.

THE SEND-OFF

Down the close, darkening lanes they sang their way
To the siding-shed,
And lined the train with faces grimly gay.

Their breasts were stuck all white with wreath and spray
As men's are, dead.

Dull porters watched them, and a casual tramp
Stood staring hard,
Sorry to miss them from the upland camp.
Then, unmoved, signals nodded, and a lamp
Winked to the guard.

So secretly, like wrongs hushed-up, they went.
They were not ours:
We never heard to which front these were sent.

Nor there if they yet mock what women meant
Who gave them flowers.

Shall they return to beatings of great bells
In wild train-loads?
A few, a few, too few for drums and yells,
May creep back, silent, to still village wells
Up half-known roads.

EXPOSURE

Our brains ache, in the merciless iced east winds that knive
  us . . .
Wearied we keep awake because the night is silent . . .
Low, drooping flares confuse our memory of the salient . . .
Worried by silence, sentries whisper, curious, nervous,
              But nothing happens.

Watching, we hear the mad gusts tugging on the wire,
Like twitching agonies of men among its brambles.
Northward, incessantly, the flickering gunnery rumbles,
Far off, like a dull rumour of some other war.
              What are we doing here?

The poignant misery of dawn begins to grow . . .
We only know war lasts, rain soaks, and clouds sag stormy.
Dawn massing in the east her melancholy army
Attacks once more in ranks on shivering ranks of gray,
              But nothing happens.

Sudden successive flights of bullets streak the silence.
Less deathly than the air that shudders black with snow,
With sidelong flowing flakes that flock, pause, and renew;
We watch them wandering up and down the wind's non-
  chalance,
              But nothing happens.

Pale flakes with fingering stealth come feeling for our
  faces –
We cringe in holes, back on forgotten dreams, and stare,
  snow-dazed,

Deep into grassier ditches. So we drowse, sun-dozed,
Littered with blossoms trickling where the blackbird fusses.
          Is it that we are dying?

Slowly our ghosts drag home: glimpsing the sunk fires,
    glozed
With crusted dark-red jewels; crickets jingle there;
For hours the innocent mice rejoice: the house is theirs;
Shutters and doors, all closed: on us the doors are closed, –
          We turn back to our dying.

Since we believe not otherwise can kind fires burn;
Nor ever suns smile true on child, or field, or fruit.
For God's invincible spring our love is made afraid;
Therefore, not loath, we lie out here; therefore were born,
          For love of God seems dying.

To-night, His frost will fasten on this mud and us,
Shrivelling many hands, puckering foreheads crisp.
The burying-party, picks and shovels in their shaking grasp,
Pause over half-known faces. All their eyes are ice,
          But nothing happens.

THE PARABLE OF THE OLD MAN
AND THE YOUNG

So Abram rose, and clave the wood, and went,
And took the fire with him, and a knife.
And as they sojourned both of them together,
Isaac the first-born spake and said, My Father,
Behold the preparations, fire and iron,
But where the lamb for this burnt-offering?
Then Abram bound the youth with belts and straps,
And builded parapets and trenches there,
And stretchèd forth the knife to slay his son.
When lo! an angel called him out of heaven,
Saying, Lay not thy hand upon the lad,
Neither do anything to him. Behold,
A ram, caught in a thicket by its horns;
Offer the Ram of Pride instead of him.
But the old man would not so, but slew his son,
And half the seed of Europe, one by one.

STRANGE MEETING

It seemed that out of battle I escaped
Down some profound dull tunnel, long since scooped
Through granites which titanic wars had groined.
Yet also there encumbered sleepers groaned,
Too fast in thought or death to be bestirred.
Then, as I probed them, one sprang up, and stared
With piteous recognition in fixed eyes,
Lifting distressful hands as if to bless.
And by his smile, I knew that sullen hall,
By his dead smile I knew we stood in Hell.
With a thousand pains that vision's face was grained;
Yet no blood reached there from the upper ground,
And no guns thumped, or down the flues made moan.
'Strange friend,' I said, 'here is no cause to mourn.'
'None,' said that other, 'save the undone years,
The hopelessness. Whatever hope is yours,
Was my life also; I went hunting wild
After the wildest beauty in the world,
Which lies not calm in eyes, or braided hair,
But mocks the steady running of the hour,
And if it grieves, grieves richlier than here.
For of my glee might many men have laughed,
And of my weeping something had been left,
Which must die now. I mean the truth untold,
The pity of war, the pity war distilled.
Now men will go content with what we spoiled,
Or, discontent, boil bloody, and be spilled.
They will be swift with swiftness of the tigress.
None will break ranks, though nations trek from progress.
Courage was mine, and I had mystery,

Wisdom was mine, and I had mastery:
To miss the march of this retreating world
Into vain citadels that are not walled.
Then, when much blood had clogged their chariot-wheels,
I would go up and wash them from sweet wells,
Even with truths that lie too deep for taint.
I would have poured my spirit without stint
But not through wounds; not on the cess of war.
Foreheads of men have bled where no wounds were.
I am the enemy you killed, my friend.
I knew you in this dark: for so you frowned
Yesterday through me as you jabbed and killed.
I parried; but my hands were loath and cold.
Let us sleep now. . . .'

GREATER LOVE

Red lips are not so red
  As the stained stones kissed by the English dead.
Kindness of wooed and wooer
Seems shame to their love pure.
O Love, your eyes lose lure
  When I behold eyes blinded in my stead!

Your slender attitude
  Trembles not exquisite like limbs knife-skewed,
Rolling and rolling there
Where God seems not to care;
Till the fierce love they bear
  Cramps them in death's extreme decrepitude.

Your voice sings not so soft, —
  Though even as wind murmuring through raftered loft,
Your dear voice is not dear,
Gentle, and evening clear,
As theirs whom none now hear,
  Now earth has stopped their piteous mouths that coughed.

Heart, you were never hot
  Nor large, nor full like hearts made great with shot;
And though your hand be pale,
Paler are all which trail
Your cross through flame and hail:
  Weep, you may weep, for you may touch them not.

ANTHEM FOR DOOMED YOUTH

What passing-bells for these who die as cattle?
  Only the monstrous anger of the guns.
  Only the stuttering rifles' rapid rattle
Can patter out their hasty orisons.
No mockeries now for them; no prayers nor bells,
  Nor any voice of mourning save the choirs, —
The shrill, demented choirs of wailing shells;
  And bugles calling for them from sad shires.

What candles may be held to speed them all?
  Not in the hands of boys, but in their eyes
Shall shine the holy glimmers of good-byes.
  The pallor of girls' brows shall be their pall;
Their flowers the tenderness of patient minds,
And each slow dusk a drawing-down of blinds.

SPRING OFFENSIVE

Halted against the shade of a last hill,
They fed, and lying easy, were at ease
And, finding comfortable chests and knees,
Carelessly slept. But many there stood still
To face the stark, blank sky beyond the ridge,
Knowing their feet had come to the end of the world.

Marvelling they stood, and watched the long grass swirled
By the May breeze, murmurous with wasp and midge,
For though the summer oozed into their veins
Like an injected drug for their bodies' pains,
Sharp on their souls hung the imminent line of grass,
Fearfully flashed the sky's mysterious glass.

Hour after hour they ponder the warm field –
And the far valley behind, where the buttercup
Had blessed with gold their slow boots coming up,
Where even the little brambles would not yield,
But clutched and clung to them like sorrowing hands;
They breathe like trees unstirred.

Till like a cold gust thrills the little word
At which each body and its soul begird
And tighten them for battle. No alarms
Of bugles, no high flags, no clamorous haste –
Only a lift and flare of eyes that faced
The sun, like a friend with whom their love is done.
O larger shone that smile against the sun, –
Mightier than his whose bounty these have spurned.

So, soon they topped the hill, and raced together
Over an open stretch of herb and heather
Exposed. And instantly the whole sky burned
With fury against them; earth set sudden cups
In thousands for their blood; and the green slope
Chasmed and steepened sheer to infinite space.

         *   *   *

Of them who running on that last high place
Leapt to swift unseen bullets, or went up
On the hot blast and fury of hell's upsurge,
Or plunged and fell away past this world's verge,
Some say God caught them even before they fell.

But what say such as from existence' brink
Ventured but drave too swift to sink,
The few who rushed in the body to enter hell,
And there out-fiending all its fiends and flames
With superhuman inhumanities,
Long-famous glories, immemorial shames –
And crawling slowly back, have by degrees
Regained cool peaceful air in wonder –
Why speak not they of comrades that went under?

DULCE ET DECORUM EST

Bent double, like old beggars under sacks,
Knock-kneed, coughing like hags, we cursed through sludge,
Till on the haunting flares we turned our backs
And towards our distant rest began to trudge.
Men marched asleep. Many had lost their boots
But limped on, blood-shod. All went lame; all blind;
Drunk with fatigue; deaf even to the hoots
Of tired, outstripped Five-Nines that dropped behind.

Gas! Gas! Quick, boys! – An ecstasy of fumbling,
Fitting the clumsy helmets just in time;
But someone still was yelling out and stumbling
And flound'ring like a man in fire or lime . . .
Dim, through the misty panes and thick green light,
As under a green sea, I saw him drowning.

In all my dreams, before my helpless sight,
He plunges at me, guttering, choking, drowning.

If in some smothering dreams you too could pace
Behind the wagon that we flung him in,
And watch the white eyes writhing in his face,
His hanging face, like a devil's sick of sin;
If you could hear, at every jolt, the blood
Come gargling from the froth-corrupted lungs,
Obscene as cancer, bitter as the cud
Of vile, incurable sores on innocent tongues, –
My friend, you would not tell with such high zest
To children ardent for some desperate glory,
The old Lie: Dulce et decorum est
Pro patria mori.

INSENSIBILITY

I

Happy are men who yet before they are killed
Can let their veins run cold.
Whom no compassion fleers
Or makes their feet
Sore on the alleys cobbled with their brothers.
The front line withers,
But they are troops who fade, not flowers
For poets' tearful fooling:
Men, gaps for filling:
Losses, who might have fought
Longer; but no one bothers.

II

And some cease feeling
Even themselves or for themselves.
Dullness best solves
The tease and doubt of shelling,
And Chance's strange arithmetic
Comes simpler than the reckoning of their shilling.
They keep no check on armies' decimation.

III

Happy are these who lose imagination:
They have enough to carry with ammunition.
Their spirit drags no pack,

Their old wounds, save with cold, can not more ache.
Having seen all things red,
Their eyes are rid
Of the hurt of the colour of blood for ever.
And terror's first constriction over,
Their hearts remain small-drawn.
Their senses in some scorching cautery of battle
Now long since ironed,
Can laugh among the dying, unconcerned.

IV

Happy the soldier home, with not a notion
How somewhere, every dawn, some men attack,
And many sighs are drained.
Happy the lad whose mind was never trained:
His days are worth forgetting more than not.
He sings along the march
Which we march taciturn, because of dusk,
The long, forlorn, relentless trend
From larger day to huger night.

V

We wise, who with a thought besmirch
Blood over all our soul,
How should we see our task
But through his blunt and lashless eyes?
Alive, he is not vital overmuch;
Dying, not mortal overmuch;
Nor sad, nor proud,
Nor curious at all.
He cannot tell
Old men's placidity from his.

VI

But cursed are dullards whom no cannon stuns,
That they should be as stones;
Wretched are they, and mean
With paucity that never was simplicity.
By choice they made themselves immune
To pity and whatever mourns in man
Before the last sea and the hapless stars;
Whatever mourns when many leave these shores;
Whatever shares
The eternal reciprocity of tears.

PHILIP LARKIN

In the autobiographical introduction Philip Larkin wrote in 1963 for a new edition of his early novel *Jill* he described his student days in Oxford in the early 1940's (he was born in 1922), his friendship there with Kingsley Amis and the enthusiasms they shared: 'Russell, Charles Ellsworth "Pee Wee" (b. 1906), clarinet and saxophone player extraordinary, was, *mutatis mutandis*, our Swinburne and our Byron. We bought every record he played on that we could find, and – literally – dreamed about similar items on the American Commodore label. ... Long afterwards, Kingsley admitted he had once sent Russell a fan letter. I said that funnily enough I had also written to Eddie Condon. We looked at each other guardedly. "Did you get an answer?" "No – did you?" "No." '

On the face of it such an enthusiasm (it is one he still retains) is unexpected in a remote and reserved poet like Larkin, who lives in Hull and works there as a librarian, whose poetry, like his literary tastes, is English to the core: 'The poetry I've enjoyed has been the kind of poetry you'd associate with me, Hardy pre-eminently, Wilfred Owen, Auden, Christina Rossetti, William Barnes; on the whole, people to whom technique seems to matter less than content, people who accept the forms they have inherited but use them to express their own content.' Yet a common chord *can* be found between those New Orleans laments, the melancholy of Hardy's poetry, and the nostalgia which lies behind so much of Larkin's own work – though the joy and affirmation present too in that early jazz is something Larkin himself recognizes and points to in his poem, 'For Sidney Bechet':

On me your voice falls as they say love should
Like an enormous yes. . . .

Those lines, and especially the phrase 'as they say', also
reveal something of Larkin's own poetic persona. 'Love' is
there, but it is held at a distance: it is not (or so one is given to
understand) something the poet has enjoyed at first hand.
Nevertheless, he is conscious of its supposed qualities and so
the (qualified) simile is allowed. It is a little harsh, therefore,
to state, as critics have, that Larkin's poetry is all negatives,
that it lacks joy, that it merely catalogues, if brilliantly, the
tedium of life, the sense of loss, of being always on the outside
– harsh, or perhaps slightly off target in that it is often the
awareness that all the supposedly positive qualities of life *are*
(or *were*) there, possessed by others, never quite coming his
way, that makes the best of Larkin's poems genuinely moving:

> The trumpet's voice, loud and authoritative,
> Draws me a moment to the lighted glass
> To watch the dancers – all under twenty-five –
> Shifting intently, face to flushed face,
> Solemnly on the beat of happiness.
>
> – Or so I fancy, sensing the smoke and sweat,
> The wonderful feel of girls. Why be out here?

These lines, from 'Reasons for Attendance', portray that other
world the poet is outside, yet he is quick to show that the
'happiness' of those scrutinized, mauling couples is not for
him, or so he would have himself believe: the word 'maul' is
deliberately used to depreciate their activity and, one sus-
pects, to give himself an out. In 'Reference Back' this same note
enters at the end, a note of desolation – or perhaps reconciliation – admittedly, yet one which *does* admit to other 'perspec-

tives' – for instance to the kind of pleasures and experiences which the first part of the poem recalls and savours:

> *That was a pretty one*, I heard you call
> From the unsatisfactory hall
> To the unsatisfactory room where I
> Played record after record, idly,
> Wasting my time at home, that you
> Looked so much forward to.

Larkin is clearly aware of the image his poems project, and has commented upon it: 'One thing I do feel a slight restiveness about is being typed as someone who has carved out for himself a uniquely dreary life, growing older, having to work, and not getting things he wants and so on – is this so different from everyone else?' In fact it is *not* so different, which is one reason why Larkin's poetry communicates so directly. Although he is obviously a learned, highly intelligent and perceptive man, his poetry is never scholarly. It is concerned with the everyday, and its power lies in its precision, in the unexpected insights it provides, in its wry self-awareness, in the areas of feeling it opens up in the reader. Above all, it is honest and unadorned, knows what it may approach and what it may not, its language never forced, its tone always easy and conversational:

> Once I am sure there's nothing going on
> I step inside, letting the door thud shut.
> Another church: matting, seats, and stone,
> And little books; sprawlings of flowers, cut
> For Sunday, brownish now; some brass and stuff
> Up at the holy end; the small neat organ;
> And a tense, musty, unignorable silence,
> Brewed God knows how long. Hatless, I take off
> My cycle-clips in awkward reverence. . . .

'Church Going', the poem from which those lines come, is the most ambitious in Larkin's fine second book, *The Less Deceived* (1955), a book which shows him to be a master of a particular kind of poem and sets him apart from the competent but generally restricted 'Movement' poets with whom he was linked and whose work has been described (by A. Alvarez in his introduction to *The New Poetry*) as 'academic-administrative verse, polite, knowledgeable, efficient, polished, and, in its quiet way, even intelligent.' Alvarez, in fact, uses the 'cycle-clip' lines of 'Church Going' to make a general point about the Movement: 'This, in concentrated form,' he says, 'is the image of the post-war Welfare State Englishman'. Maybe, but the poem has exceptional intrinsic qualities (as I'm sure Alvarez would grant) which make it much more than that. The image of the little man awkwardly entering the vast church, taking courage, fooling a little, retreating into silence and sonorous observation – all this is carried brilliantly by the form and tone of the verse as it moves easily through its various gears to the ceremonial ending. (When asked in an interview whether he saw 'Church Going' as a debate between poet and persona, Larkin replied: 'Well, in a way. The poem starts by saying, you don't really know about all this, you don't believe it, you don't know what a rood-loft is – Why do you come here, why do you bother to stop and look around? The poem is seeking an answer. I suppose that's the antithesis you mean. I think one has to dramatize oneself a little. I don't arse about in churches when I'm alone. Not much, anyway. I still don't know what rood-lofts are.')

The strong narrative facility displayed in that poem is seen again in the title-poem of Larkin's most recent book, *The Whitsun Weddings* (1964). Like Thomas Hardy he knows how to encapsulate and make memorable in verse form a compelling story; and memorable indeed is that train ride, the families waving from the platform to the newly-weds, the sad, tinselled gaiety of it all. Here, as in many Larkin poems, a person is seen in, or is projected into, a dramatic situation: here, as always, the description and lead-up are compelling, the (in this case erotic) climax unexpected, yet right:

> . . . We slowed again,
> And as the tightened brakes took hold, there swelled
> A sense of falling, like an arrow-shower
> Sent out of sight, somewhere becoming rain.

It is often said that Larkin's poetry lacks emotion, but the poems themselves argue a different case, even spilling on rare occasions into sentimentality. The attitude to sex they display has been described as 'old-maidenish' yet in fact the emotional punch often comes from the understatement itself: one cannot but be aware of a conflict between the conscious will to keep coolly distant and the unconscious desire to approach, to become involved; and of the resultant tension, straining beneath the calm surface of the verse. This tension is evident in the best of *The Whitsun Weddings* poems, though occassionally Larkin does seem to have removed many of the possibilities, to have sorted everything out just too neatly. Thus in the poem 'Ambulances' one is halted by the doom-laden, bland, albeit unarguable conclusion:

> Closed like confessionals, they thread
> Loud noons of cities, giving back
> None of the glances they absorb.
> Light glossy grey, arms on a plaque,
> They come to rest at any kerb:
> All streets in time are visited.

There are, though, wonderful exceptions – poems like 'Broadcast' or 'Love Songs in Age' – and it would be wrong, with a poet of Larkin's calibre, to over-emphasize the point and force conclusions, or to overlook the wit and tenderness he so often displays.

The final point I would like to make about Larkin's poetry is simply that it is *enjoyable*: one is conscious of being in the presence of a craftsman who is in perfect control of his technique, who knows what he wants to say, and who says it perfectly – a rare enough experience. Sometimes too, as in the poem 'At Grass', the lines themselves attain a rightness and beauty which defies definition. Larkin may not be a great experimenter, but he has chosen his beat and he covers it with unrivalled authority. As Alvarez has put it, 'without posturing or pretence he has done something in poetry which is quite his own and quite undeniable.'

Philip Larkin writes:

. . . Some years ago I came to the conclusion that to write a poem was to construct a verbal device that would preserve an experience indefinitely by reproducing it in whoever read the poem. As a working definition, this satisfied me sufficiently to enable individual poems to be written. In so far as it suggested that all one had to do was pick an experience and preserve it, however, it was much over-simplified. Nowadays nobody believes in 'poetic' subjects, any more than they believe in poetic diction. The longer one goes on, though, the more one feels that some subjects are more poetic than others, if only that poems about them get written whereas poems about other subjects don't. At first one tries to write poems about everything. Later on, one learns to distinguish somewhat, though one can still make enormously time wasting mistakes. The fact is that my working definition defines very little: it makes no reference to this necessary element of distinction, and it leaves the precise nature of the verbal pickling unexplained.

This means that most of the time one is engaged in doing, or trying to do, something of which the value is doubtful and the mode of operation unclear. Can one feel entirely happy about this? The days when one could claim to be the priest of a mystery are gone: today mystery means either ignorance or hokum, neither fashionable qualities. Yet writing a poem is still not an act of the will. The distinction between subjects is not an act of the will. Whatever makes a poem successful is not an act of the will. In consequence, the poems that actually get written may seem trivial or unedifying, compared with those that don't. But the poems that get written, even if they do not please the will, evidently please that mysterious something that has to be pleased.

This is not to say that one is forever writing poems of which the will disapproves. What it does mean, however, is that there must be among the ingredients that go towards the writing of a poem a streak of curious self gratification, almost impossible to describe except in some such terms, the presence of which tends to nullify any satisfaction the will might be feeling at a finished job. . . . The only consolation in the whole business, as in just about every other, is that in all probability there was really no choice.

From the *Poetry Book Society Bulletin*.

REASONS FOR ATTENDANCE

The trumpet's voice, loud and authoritative,
Draws me a moment to the lighted glass
To watch the dancers – all under twenty-five –
Shifting intently, face to flushed face,
Solemnly on the beat of happiness.

– Or so I fancy, sensing the smoke and sweat,
The wonderful feel of girls. Why be out here?
But then, why be in there? Sex, yes, but what
Is sex? Surely, to think the lion's share
Of happiness is found by couples – sheer

Inaccuracy, as far as I'm concerned.
What calls me is that lifted, rough-tongued bell
(Art, if you like) whose individual sound
Insists I too am individual.
It speaks; I hear; others may hear as well,

But not for me, nor I for them; and so
With happiness. Therefore I stay outside,
Believing this; and they maul to and fro,
Believing that; and both are satisfied,
If no one has misjudged himself. Or lied.

CHURCH GOING

Once I am sure there's nothing going on
I step inside, letting the door thud shut.
Another church: matting, seats, and stone,
And little books; sprawlings of flowers, cut
For Sunday, brownish now; some brass and stuff
Up at the holy end; the small neat organ;
And a tense, musty, unignorable silence,
Brewed God knows how long. Hatless, I take off
My cycle-clips in awkward reverence,

Move forward, run my hand around the font.
From where I stand, the roof looks almost new –
Cleaned, or restored? Someone would know: I don't.
Mounting the lectern, I peruse a few
Hectoring large-scale verses, and pronounce
'Here endeth' much more loudly than I'd meant.
The echoes snigger briefly. Back at the door
I sign the book, donate an Irish sixpence,
Reflect the place was not worth stopping for.

Yet stop I did: in fact I often do,
And always end much at a loss like this,
Wondering what to look for; wondering, too,
When churches fall completely out of use
What we shall turn them into, if we shall keep
A few cathedrals chronically on show,
Their parchment, plate and pyx in locked cases,
And let the rest rent-free to rain and sheep.
Shall we avoid them as unlucky places?

Or, after dark, will dubious women come
To make their children touch a particular stone;
Pick simples for a cancer; or on some
Advised night see walking a dead one?
Power of some sort or other will go on
In games, in riddles, seemingly at random;
But superstition, like belief, must die,
And what remains when disbelief has gone?
Grass, weedy pavement, brambles, buttress, sky,

A shape less recognizable each week,
A purpose more obscure. I wonder who
Will be the last, the very last, to seek
This place for what it was; one of the crew
That tap and jot and know what rood-lofts were?
Some ruin-bibber, randy for antique,
Or Christmas-addict, counting on a whiff
Of gown-and-bands and organ-pipes and myrrh?
Or will he be my representative,

Bored, uninformed, knowing the ghostly silt
Dispersed, yet tending to this cross of ground
Through suburb scrub because it held unspilt
So long and equably what since is found
Only in separation – marriage, and birth,
And death, and thoughts of these – for whom was built
This special shell? For, though I've no idea
What this accoutred frowsty barn is worth,
It pleases me to stand in silence here;

A serious house on serious earth it is,
In whose blent air all our compulsions meet,
Are recognized, and robed as destinies.
And that much never can be obsolete,
Since someone will forever be surprising

A hunger in himself to be more serious,
And gravitating with it to this ground,
Which, he once heard, was proper to grow wise in,
If only that so many dead lie round.

AT GRASS

The eye can hardly pick them out
From the cold shade they shelter in,
Till wind distresses tail and mane;
Then one crops grass, and moves about
– The other seeming to look on –
And stands anonymous again.

Yet fifteen years ago, perhaps
Two dozen distances sufficed
To fable them: faint afternoons
Of Cups and Stakes and Handicaps,
Whereby their names were artificed
To inlay faded, classic Junes –

Silks at the start: against the sky
Numbers and parasols: outside,
Squadrons of empty cars, and heat,
And littered grass: then the long cry
Hanging unhushed till it subside
To stop-press columns on the street.

Do memories plague their ears like flies?
They shake their heads. Dusk brims the shadows.
Summer by summer all stole away,
The starting-gates, the crowds and cries –
All but the unmolesting meadows.
Almanacked, their names live; they

Have slipped their names, and stand at ease,
Or gallop for what must be joy,

And not a fieldglass sees them home,
Or curious stop-watch prophesies:
Only the groom, and the groom's boy,
With bridles in the evening come.

BROADCAST

Giant whispering and coughing from
Vast Sunday-full and organ-frowned-on spaces
Precede a sudden scuttle on the drum,
'The Queen', and huge resettling. Then begins
A snivel on the violins:
I think of your face among all those faces,

Beautiful and devout before
Cascades of monumental slithering,
One of your gloves unnoticed on the floor
Beside those new, slightly-outmoded shoes.
Here it goes quickly dark. I lose
All but the outline of the still and withering

Leaves on half-emptied trees. Behind
The glowing wavebands, rabid storms of chording
By being distant overpower my mind
All the more shamelessly, their cut-off shout
Leaving me desperate to pick out
Your hands, tiny in all that air, applauding.

REFERENCE BACK

That was a pretty one, I heard you call
From the unsatisfactory hall
To the unsatisfactory room where I
Played record after record, idly,
Wasting my time at home, that you
Looked so much forward to.

Oliver's *Riverside Blues*, it was. And now
I shall, I suppose, always remember how
The flock of notes those antique negroes blew
Out of Chicago air into
A huge remembering pre-electric horn
The year after I was born
Three decades later made this sudden bridge
From your unsatisfactory age
To my unsatisfactory prime.

Truly, though our element is time,
We are not suited to the long perspectives
Open at each instant of our lives.
They link us to our losses: worse,
They show us what we have as it once was,
Blindingly undiminished, just as though
By acting differently we could have kept it so.

LOVE SONGS IN AGE

She kept her songs, they took so little space,
  The covers pleased her:
One bleached from lying in a sunny place,
One marked in circles by a vase of water,
One mended, when a tidy fit had seized her,
  And coloured, by her daughter –
So they had waited, till in widowhood
She found them, looking for something else, and stood

Relearning how each frank submissive chord
  Had ushered in
Word after sprawling hyphenated word,
And the unfailing sense of being young
Spread out like a spring-woken tree, wherein
  That hidden freshness sung,
That certainty of time laid up in store
As when she played them first. But, even more,

The glare of that much-mentioned brilliance, love,
  Broke out, to show
Its bright incipience sailing above,
Still promising to solve, and satisfy,
And set unchangeably in order. So
  To pile them back, to cry,
Was hard, without lamely admitting how
It had not done so then, and could not now.

THE CARDPLAYERS

Jan van Hogspeuw staggers to the door
And pisses at the dark. Outside, the rain
Courses in cart-ruts down the deep mud lane.
Inside, Dirk Dogstoerd pours himself some more,
And holds a cinder to his clay with tongs,
Belching out smoke. Old Prijck snores with the gale,
His skull face firelit; someone behind drinks ale,
And opens mussels, and croaks scraps of songs
Towards the ham-hung rafters about love.
Dirk deals the cards. Wet century-wide trees
Clash in surrounding starlessness above
This lamplit cave, where Jan turns back and farts,
Gobs at the grate, and hits the queen of hearts.

Rain, wind and fire! The secret, bestial peace!

DUBLINESQUE

Down stucco sidestreets,
Where light is pewter
And afternoon mist
Brings lights on in shops
Above race-guides and rosaries,
A funeral passes.

The hearse is ahead,
But after there follows
A troop of streetwalkers
In wide flowered hats,
Leg-of-mutton sleeves,
And ankle-length dresses.

There is an air of great friendliness,
As if they were honouring
One they were fond of;
Some caper a few steps,
Skirts held skilfully
(Someone claps time),

And of great sadness also.
As they wend away
A voice is heard singing
Of Kitty, or Katy,
As if the name meant once
All love, all beauty.

SAD STEPS

Groping back to bed after a piss
I part thick curtains, and am startled by
The rapid clouds, the moon's cleanliness.

Four o'clock: wedge-shadowed gardens lie
Under a cavernous, a wind-picked sky.
There's something laughable about this,

The way the moon dashes through clouds that blow
Loosely as cannon-smoke to stand apart
(Stone-coloured light sharpening the roofs below)

High and preposterous and separate –
Lozenge of love! Medallion of art!
O wolves of memory! Immensements! No,

One shivers slightly, looking up there.
The hardness and the brightness and the plain
Far-reaching singleness of that wide stare

Is a reminder of the strength and pain
Of being young; that it can't come again,
But is for others undiminished somewhere.

TO THE SEA

To step over the low wall that divides
Road from concrete walk above the shore
Brings sharply back something known long before –
The miniature gaiety of seasides.
Everything crowds under the low horizon:
Steep beach, blue water, towels, red bathing caps,
The small hushed waves' repeated fresh collapse
Up the warm yellow sand, and further off
A white steamer stuck in the afternoon –

Still going on, all of it, still going on!
To lie, eat, sleep in hearing of the surf
(Ears to transistors, that sound tame enough
Under the sky), or gently up and down
Lead the uncertain children, frilled in white
And grasping at enormous air, or wheel
The rigid old along for them to feel
A final summer, plainly still occurs
As half an annual pleasure, half a rite,

As when, happy at being on my own,
I searched the sand for Famous Cricketers,
Or, farther back, my parents, listeners
To the same seaside quack, first became known.
Strange to it now, I watch the cloudless scene:
The same clear water over smoothed pebbles,
The distant bathers' weak protesting trebles
Down at its edge, and then the cheap cigars,
The chocolate-papers, tea-leaves, and, between

The rocks, the rusting soup-tins, till the first
Few families start the trek back to the cars.
The white steamer has gone. Like breathed-on glass
The sunlight has turned milky. If the worst
Of flawless weather is our falling short,
It may be that through habit these do best,
Coming to water clumsily undressed
Yearly; teaching their children by a sort
Of clowning; helping the old, too, as they ought.

THOMAS BLACKBURN

THOMAS BLACKBURN was born in Cumberland in 1916, the son of a country vicar. In his autobiographical book, *A Clip of Steel*, he recreates the stultifying atmosphere of the Victorian home he grew up in, a home dominated by the gargantuan figure of his father Elial: 'I remember with photographic clarity our wild chases around tables and chairs. The outcome was always the same; I would be lugged, kicking and roaring, into his study, and there, under two paintings of Jesus by some lugubrious German, Elial would lam into me with the weighty strop with which he administered justice and sharpened his razor.'

The steel clip of Mr. Blackburn's title refers to an instrument sent to him at boarding school by his father to prevent nocturnal erections, just one of many spiked devices – physical and mental – with which a sex-fearing, sex-obsessed father sought to direct his all too frail and human son along virtue's path. If sex was Mr. Blackburn Senior's main obsession, colour ran it a close second. Born in Mauritius, where his grandfather landed with the British army in 1810, Elial inherited from *his* father a haunting fear of things 'dark'. Thus he was filled with shame and alarm by what he alone took to be his son's less than lilly-whiteness. Indeed one of Thomas Blackburn's most vivid early memories is of waking to find his face being scraped with peroxide and lemon juice!

Blackburn's struggle through this maze of taboos towards self-expression led him in many directions, his weapons against the horrors being an inventive devilishness which shocked teachers and doctors alike and drove his doting mother to despair. When he came to write poetry it is hardly surprising that his subject-matter should stem to some considerable degree from those traumatic early battles – battles which he seems still to be fighting in his verse: the two paintings of Christ, and their associations with the strop, with Germany, with physical violence, are never far from his mind.

What poets write about the nature of poetry often throws revealing light on their work, and in his critical book, *The Price of An Eye*, Blackburn wrote: 'It is within the darkness of himself that he [the poet] confronts the powers of imagination. . . . The poet may not lapse into the unknown darkness. He brings it into the light of his mind; through his work he gives its creatures a local habitation and a name, and so relates them to the business of daily life.' That phrase, 'the business of daily life', goes some way towards indicating the kind of experience given habitation in Thomas Blackburn's own poetry, and which in the best of it, is made actual in a quite riveting way. Often the poet appears to be engaged in a kind of dialogue with some dead or living person with whom he is at war. Yet for all this his early poems are surprisingly restrained, echoing (as he would acknowledge) the music and cadence of Yeats. Nevertheless, the sureness of touch is impressive. What's more, a lively and resourceful mind was clearly at work – and once the individuality broke through the Yeatsian shackles (in such poems as 'Lord of the Images' and 'Pasiphaë') the power and virtuosity quickly made themselves felt. By the time *The Next Word* was published in 1958, the *Times Literary Supplement* could justly write of him as one of the 'most technically accomplished poets of his generation'. By this time too the areas of his concern had crystalized. Describing them in the *Sunday Times*, John Press wrote: 'His concern is with the deepest experiences of mankind – the wounds of childhood, the pleasures and inadequacies of carnal love, the need for sacrifice.'

The music evident in the early volumes has remained, but the tune has changed. *A Smell of Burning*, published in 1961, shows this clearly. The vocabulary is generally more violent, with words like 'hounds', 'claws', 'savage' and 'hysterical' pervading. Gradually the dialogue has become a monologue. The poet, one feels, is presenting *his* side of a case – whether to his reader, to some ambiguous God-figure, or to himself. Indeed, he would often appear to be in conversation with himself and the most successful of the poems seem to have articulated completely some inner need, to have come to terms with themselves, to have found repose through and in the poetry. 'For a Child' is one poem from this volume which achieves such equipoise.

As an educationalist, and the editor of various anthologies and handbooks for teachers, Thomas Blackburn is acutely conscious of the function of poetry and of the need in writing it to communicate and interest the reader – and yet, at the same time, aware too of the impossibility of compromise, of the rigours and disciplines which go into the making of a poem. This paradox is expressed strongly in a poem called 'An Invitation', in which he contemplates an invitation to read his poems 'for a decent fee':

What I can confirm is the struggle that never lets up
Between the horses of Plato beneath my yoke,
One after Light, and for Hell not giving a rap,
The other only keen on infernal smoke.
And poems. . . ? From time to time they commemorate
Some particularly dirty battle between the two;
I put the letter down – what's the right tone?
'Dear Sir', I type, 'how nice to speak to you!'

That colloquial ending is perhaps indicative of the altogether looser, more down-to-earth approach that was to emerge in *A Breathing Space* (1964). 'A Small Keen Wind' projects the 'new' Blackburn voice at its most engaging. The dark, icy music, the carefully balanced words, the gradually accelerating rhythms are charged with indignation, self-awareness, strain. However, at the end, in the last four lines, the storm which sparked the whole thing off gives way to a calmer passage as the poem moves outside its domestic situation to catch a moment of mystery:

> I saw tonight – walking to cool the mind –
> A little moonshine on a garden wall
> And, as I brooded, felt a small, keen wind
> Stroll from the Arctic at its own sweet will.

Oddly, *A Breathing Space* was treated unkindly by various critics, some pointing to Yeats, others to Browning, and all but a few missing a cluster of poems of unusual penetration, 'Teaching Wordsworth', 'A Point of Honour' and 'En Route' among them. There is no denying that some uneven, quixotic poems are included in the volume, just as some were in its predecessor, and that even in a successful poem like 'En Route' there are strange inversions. But it falls to the real artist to turn such quirks of style to his advantage, and in this poem Thomas Blackburn does so impressively, the chilling flow of the verse as it moves to its climax sweeping all before it:

> And at long last no debt was owed
> Since on my shoulders lay the road.

Perhaps the book was too individual for some tastes, perhaps too honest. Certainly it was (to quote Blackburn's own phrase on Wordsworth) concerned with 'life's outgoing towards death'; certainly the poems were firmly rooted in the life of their author – concerned, as they were, with the break-up of one marriage and the celebration of another, with identity, and with an examination of the minutae which constitute life on earth. But even at their most intense they contain a dry, debunking (often self-debunking) wit. 'Teaching Wordsworth', ostensibly the least personal of poems, provides an interesting example:

> 'Our theme today is the poet, Wordsworth
> Who, since not alive still, I disinter
> For the sake of a question you will answer,
> For the sake also of the vagrant lives
> He was involved with, and the wind when it raves
> Round such unmarketable places as Scawfell.
> An unsociable man and often dull . . .'

No pretensions here, and no dullness. A sharp pin pricks the Wordsworthian balloon and makes the poet human again. In Blackburn's poetry everything is related to the human, and this is as true of the mythological poems as it is of those which explore religious themes. The remarkable thing is that the struggle and tensions behind the poetry increase, as his latest volume, *The Fourth Man* (1971) shows. By now his identification with such tortured artists as Beethoven, Baudelaire and Van Gogh is complete ('All the Immortals'). What strikes one also is the way religious imagery and associations are now woven quite naturally into the structure of secular poems, just as twentieth-century images and terms of reference and speech are part of the 'religious' ones.

It is hard to predict the future direction of Thomas Blackburn's work: his latest book contains two unusually long poems and novel-writing now absorbs much of his creative energy. This unpredictability is attractive. Even when most flippant (and sometimes *especially* then) his poems always entertain, are always direct and readable: one knows he is playing the *enfant terrible* or eccentric don, or perhaps cocking a snook at some critic or phantom. As an outspoken man, with no time for fashion or its proponents, he has shunned in the past year or two the British periodicals, hitting out at their insularity and sameness. Thus his newer poems have not had the audience they deserve. This is the reading public's loss, for when the targets are in focus, and the voice tuned, his poems attain a dramatic stature rare in modern verse.

Thomas Blackburn writes:

First of all I wanted to talk about my own problems through myths, Oedipus for example, and Pasiphaë; I only got excited by those great themes because they touched off something in myself. They were a kind of bridge between myself and the audience. But later I wanted to write very much more directly about what went on in my own life. But I suppose that one's life is a kind of myth, that one is lived by things, written by things, almost beyond one's control. I wanted in my last two books to make poetry about everyday experiences and show how they touch off into all sorts of mysterious areas and significances. Quite little things like a quarrel or watching birds from a stone by the sea, can arouse innumerable echoes . . .

I feel that Christianity is still there, but now it is bursting through the seams of churches and orthodoxy and that we have somehow to take the characters of its divine drama, Judas, Christ, etc., and bring them back inside ourselves, into the Armageddon of the human being himself . . .

If you could get your own private devils exorcised I feel that you would be doing something for society, because if you manage to come clean of these various things then the way you react to society would be quite different, wouldn't it? I find no difference between the clarification, elucidation and understanding of one's own personal problems and those of society. After all, one is busy with society and the reaction one has depends on how much one has understood oneself . . .

I get an idea, a sort of germ comes, and if that comes I know the poem will be finished. But it may take me weeks and weeks of brooding and thinking about this exciting idea, and then suddenly the poem will arrive; but it takes a long period of gestation; then once the birthpoint has been reached the thing is written quickly; but then comes the working over and that's a long process. ... When you write a poem you must feel the absolute value of the writing, you brush away all other considerations but the poem. This is supremely important and the whole of your energy must be, as it were, offered like a kind of sacrifice to the poem.

(From a broadcast interview September 3, 1964)

As one gets rather older the questions remain but the answers become more difficult to find. Some years ago I would not have found it difficult to say why I write poetry. I might have said, because I have some conflict or problem which cannot be solved except by that third thing which is the poem, or that poetry is the way some problem shoulders up into the light of day, some problem which has been just under the surface of consciousness.

Probably those remarks still have some truth to them but now I prefer to say I write poetry because I have to. There is some energy of myself which can only find its proper satisfaction by making a poem. Why this should be so is now beyond my ability to answer. But I do know that the need exists, that it is an occasional visitor, and that when it comes it brings stress and some degree of turmoil, growing pains, but that I would not be without its imperious need to express itself through me as a poem.

(Spring, 1971)

PASIPHAË

Tonight that thirsting girl glides through the town,
With nervous footsteps from the royal door,
Crushed ivy, liquid music in her mouth,
To mate a beast upon the sea's cold shore.

White on the salted margin she lies down,
'Darkness, now take me, now, Darkness'; she sighs.
Slowly it breeds upon her, throbs, grows full,
The spirit carnal in a panting bull,
Straddles her body with its heavy thighs.

The morning breaks; upon the trampled sand,
Blood crusted to her side, foam in her hair,
She drops blue pebbles from an idle hand,
Sunlight reflected in her calm blank stare.

And then they find her; she can't speak at all,
Giggles and points her tongue, she plays bo-peep,
Crawls crab-like on the earth, begins to weep,
Blasted and burnt out like a terminal.

Fused, the mind broken; how could she that stress
Of loaded voltage, beating hammer blows,
Redeem with her untutored nakedness?
It craved the pattern of a psychic rose,
Steel-petalled, to transform its savage need
To hallowed energy; well, some must bleed.
I like to think they took her home to rest,
Wiped her quite clean and fed her, till that day,
Matted with ochre fur, the man-beast lay
And whimpered naked on her childish breast.

A SMELL OF BURNING

After each savage, hysterical episode,
So common with us, my mother would sniff the air
And murmur, 'Nurse, would you look at the upstairs fire,
I smell burning, something's alight somewhere.'
But a red coal never was found, or jet of gas,
Scorching dry board, or paint-work beginning to melt;
And too young was I in that nursery time to guess
What smoking, subjective fire she really smelt.
Nowadays I know quite well from hers they came,
And my father's mouth, when the hot tongues crackled
    and spat;
But what mattered then was a trick of dodging flame,
And keeping some breath alive in the heat of it.
I have it still, that inbred dodging trick;
But always – when fire-beset – I see them turning,
My parents, to name elsewhere their sour fire reek,
And touch myself and know what's really burning.

HOSPITAL FOR DEFECTIVES

By your unnumbered charities
A miracle disclose,
Lord of the Images, whose love
The eyelid and the rose
Takes for a language, and today
Tell to me what is said
By these men in a turnip field
And their unleavened bread.

For all things seem to figure out
The stirrings of your heart,
And two men pick the turnips up
And two men pull the cart;
And yet between the four of them
No word is ever said.
Because the yeast was not put in
Which makes the human bread.
But three men stare on vacancy
And one man strokes his knees;
What is the meaning to be found
In such dark vowels as these?

Lord of the Images, whose love
The eyelid and the rose
Takes for a metaphor, today,
Beneath the warder's blows,
The unleavened man did not cry out
Or turn his face away;
Through such men in a turnip field
What is it that you say?

A POINT OF HONOUR

IN MEMORY OF ADELAIDE BLACKBURN. 1876–1962

You bequeathed no memorial,
But gave your body and your eyes away,
Wishing unto the last to be serviceable.
Your ashes, you said, must be scattered on Brighton bay
But no stone must perpetuate the trivial
Minutiae of old age that every day
Encroached on your possibilities of freedom,
Till cancer decided you could not even throw
Bread for the winter birds, or walk at random
With your companions of sunlight and casual snow.

It was snowing hard when they came to take you,
And I am told how anxious you were to dress
Neatly, yourself; it was a point of honour
To walk upright away, with your distress
Borne on your own and no one else's shoulder,
To bear with dignity your proper cross.
And then for sixteen days you were in labour,
But for yourself this time, and not for us,
Your children, who held your hand as it got darker,
As death grew large for you, but our sun less.

It is your puzzled look that I remember,
As almost gone, you caught a glimpse of me
Haunting your bedside, now a ghostly stranger
From the live world your eyes learnt not to see,
As slowly you drew from us to another
And breathless mode of being, beyond speech,

Working each night and day a little further
From sight and taste and smell and human touch,
Till you exchanged mortality, my mother,
For a new world your children could not reach.

But lying there at the end, in conversation
No longer with myself – but with the dead? –
I caught your words with interest and compassion
And when 'She's wandering' the Sister said,
Thought, Yes, but with whom? for I felt on someone
Not given to my sense you attended.

And then the talking stopped. Though they continued,
Your lungs – and terribly – to labour on,
They were alone now, for the one who used them
Out of those sodden animals had gone:
So when I stood at last for the committal
Of you to death, your sediment to fire,
I did not feel the need for lamentation
Or the irrelevance of formal prayer,
Only of going on a little further
In knowledge of our dark predicament;
I think this was for you a point of honour,
And what you never said but always meant.

FOR A CHILD

And have I put upon your shoulders then,
What in myself I have refused to bear,
My own and the confusion of dead men,
You of all these, my daughter, made my heir,
The furies and the griefs of which I stayed
Quite unaware?

Perhaps because I did not with my tongue
State these sharp energies into the mind,
They are the shadows you grow up among;
You suffer darkness because I was blind,
Take up the chaosses that in myself
Were unconfined.

If I should say, I also know the tart
Flavour of other men, as my excuse,
And took into myself their broken heart,
That's not the point, abuse remains abuse;
May chaos though have light within your mind,
And be of use.

EN ROUTE

It's strange, I thought, though half now stretches
Behind my back, how this road clutches
To its small grit and measuring stone,
Still more of life as I walk on;
Must all directions be subdued
By the compulsion of the road?

And strange it is, since there're no fences,
I do not take the path which glances
Aside from this, as if one strict
Intention gathered up all fact;
Is it because I'm whittled down
To the sharp stones I journey on?

Once certainly the traveller hurried
Down every path the wind unburied.
Finding, however, each new search
Swung back to the old line of march,
And that through detours I could not
Bypass myself or the road's grit,

Though still a side-lane light discloses,
I would hold back from its green mazes,
Sensing, though light it may reflect,
Once entered it would be blunt fact,
And so a double tax be owed
To the compulsion of the road.

Not that today they do not differ,
Myself and the relentless pressure

Of gravel underneath my feet,
But now I glimpse I half beget,
Step after step, what I walk on,
And know I am the origin

Of so much love and hate which gathers
Round those who with me are wayfarers.
Perhaps when to myself, the dreamer,
I wake, and understand the ardour
In which all burn, more clear I'll know
Who others are, myself also,

Than when it seemed far off, the fever
Which shakes me now. Since doom and glamour
No man can fly from or possess,
By stillness I make good their loss,
And find, upon the edge of winter,
More plain the way, as light grows fainter.

Last night I dreamt the road diminished
To a last stone, and where it perished
I met a child beside a river,
Who asked if I would bear him over.
I knelt then as if asking pardon,
But on my back his little burden

Than the whole world became much greater,
As stepping down into the water
I braced myself to find what could
Sustain my feet when I was dead,
And at long last no debt was owed
Since on my shoulders lay the road.

A SMALL KEEN WIND

My wife for six months now in sinister
Tones has muttered incessantly about divorce,
And, since of the woman I'm fond, this dark chatter
Is painful as well as a bit monotonous.
Still, marvel one must, when she fishes out of that trunk,
Like rags, my shadier deeds for all to see
With 'This you did when sober, and that when drunk',
At the remarkable powers of memory.
For although I wriggle like mad when she whistles up
Some particularly nasty bit of handiwork,
The dirty linen I simply cannot drop,
Since 'Thomas Blackburn' is stitched by the laundry mark.
So I gather the things and say, 'Yes, these are mine,
Though some cleaner items are not upon your list',
Then walk with my bundle of rags to another room
Since I will not play the role of delinquent ghost
And be folded up by guilt in the crook of an arm.
I saw tonight – walking to cool the mind –
A little moonshine on a garden wall
And, as I brooded, felt a small, keen wind
Stroll from the Arctic at its own sweet will.

TEACHING WORDSWORTH

FOR ALEX AND IRENE EVANS

'I'm paid to speak, and money glosses
Irrelevance; to keep their places
Students are paid, and so the burden
Is lightened of our mutual boredom,
And if the gain's not much, the damage
Is also slight within this college.

'Since for the most part it's subjective,
Verse is not anything you might have
In hand or a bank, although it is
Important to some (it is on our syllabus)
Concerned with life's outgoing towards death.
Our theme today is the poet Wordsworth.

'Who, since not alive still, I disinter
For the sake of a question you will answer,
For the sake also of the vagrant lives
He was involved with, and the wind when it raves
Round such unmarketable places as Scawfell.
An unsociable man and often dull,

'He lived for a long time posthumous
To the "flashing shield", to the poet he was,
Busy for the most part with pedestrian exercise;
However you will not be questioned on those days,
Only the time when with stone footfall
Crags followed him, winds blew through his long skull.

'That, of course, is known as "the Great Period".
Though one hesitates to apply the word "God"
To a poet's theme – it is so manhandled –
Gentlemen, I can offer you nothing instead;
If he himself never applied it to what occurred
When "the light of sense went out", this useful word
Though inaccurate will cut my lecture short,
Being the full-stop which ends thought

'And consequently for our purpose useful;
For its brevity you should be grateful.
Anyway for those who "know" what the man meant,
My words are – thanks to God – irrelevant.
"Take notes" is the advice I bequeath the rest;
It is a question of self-interest,

'Of being, as Shakespeare says, "to oneself true",
Since the right marks will certainly benefit you.
After all, in the teaching world exam and thesis
For the better posts provide a sound basis,
And in this sense poems are as good as money.
This man's life was a strange journey.

'Early deprived of both father and mother,
To the rocks he turned, to lapping water,
With a sense by deprivation made so acute
That he heard grass speak and the word in a stone's throat;
Many, of course, to silence address their prayer,
But in his case when he spoke it chose to answer,

'And he wrote down, after a certain time-lag,
Their conversation. It is a dialogue
Almost unique in any literature
And a positive gold-mine to the commentator,

For although his words mention what silence said
It can almost any way be interpreted,

'Since to find a yardstick by which the occult
Language of stones can be measured is difficult,
Also that "something far more deeply interfused"
Must be belittled by critiques, if not abused,
There being no instrument with which to measure
This origin of terms and formula

'Which, together with the birth and deathward aim
Of the life in us and things, was this man's theme
As he drew and dwindled into a worse
End of life (as regards verse).
My conclusion is: most words do violence
To what he said. Listen to silence.'

SCHIARA*

No petal has moved or feather
This day of heat without wind
Of the tamarisk and mimosa
And now they earthward bend
For the catharsis of thunder
That broods and gathers up there
In the cauldron of Schiara,
A potency of fire.

Your head lies on my shoulder,
Sweating because of the heat,
Last night in the dusk from La Stanga
We came to a mountain hut,
And made peace with a hunger
On wine and meat and bread,
Which though it continues forever
Still needs such common good.

Since meeting is knowing, and meeting
Is knowing we understand
So little, under Schiara,
This night of heat but no wind,
For the catharsis of thunder
Wait with me world without end.

* Schiara—mountains in the Italian Dolomites.

74

A BROKEN IMAGE

Walking in the Alps, my wife and I
Found a broken cross half buried under
A fall of rock and turf and red scree.

Since it came away, the figure
Of Christ, easily from its rusted
Nail, under a worm-eaten, weather

Worn image of wood we transported
From Italy without permission
We drink our wine now, eat our daily bread.

Since friends who come here often mention
The great skill of an anonymous
Carver of beech-wood, the conversation

Is enriched by this being with us
As at Cana, I'd say, if the bowed head
With any locality or surface

Chatter could be associated.
Leaning forward, as it does, from our wall,
To where silence is concentrated

Outside and within the ephemeral
Constellations of energy,
Because it says nothing reasonable

This image explains nothing away
And just by gazing into darkness
Is able to mean more than words can say.

LAUDANUM

For a raging tooth, a bad cold or neuralgia
It was prescribed constantly and thought benevolent
By many eminent professors of Medicare;
Mind you, as regards children, to sleep full
Of Mother Bailey's Spirit or McMum's Elixir,
Though good for dinner parties, could be lethal –
And often was. For the poor, cheaper than gin,
It relieved the pain of being human
Under inhuman conditions. Wealthier poetic men
Whether the stimulus was cholera or insomnia
Celebrated their first rapport like a honeymoon;
Ecstatic visions rewarded the enquirer
In a passive sense, for the most part, beautiful
Enough in itself. The mooned and poppied water
The basin of the mind itself could fill
And dispense with the ardour of the creator,
Only from far off the dumb, blind waiter
Groped from eternity to present the bill.

ALL THE IMMORTALS

Walking, catlike, between the imperatives,
Battering against iron bars and wood and stone,
Staring red-eyed through all correlatives
Into the heart of 'Being', and their own,
I think of those who found it hard to be human –
Beethoven raging, splintered within his head
The intolerable details of 'correct' behaviour,
While to enter his brain and be interpreted
Yearned a celestial but disordered order;
Baudelaire coupling on a dirty bed
With the antithesis of his Beata,
'Pour contempler mon coeur . . . et sans dégoût,
Seigneur, donnez moi la force et le courage',
That Dutchman posting off his severed ear,
Swift stalking through his intolerable dotage,
The mob's delight, spectacle and spectre;
'All the Immortals' Yeats said, and all the Immortals,
Their salt-cut hands, their broken eyes that stare
Through the minute particulars of knowledge
Into the daemon of phenomena,
Who else these Lenten days should one remember?

KEITH DOUGLAS

WHEN Keith Douglas was killed in Normandy in 1944, just before 'D' Day, he left behind a body of work which marked him out (in the words of the *Horizon* critic) as the only young poet 'who has written poems comparable with the works of the better poets of the last war.' However, to label Douglas a war poet in this way is to limit and misrepresent the nature of his achievement, for though he wrote his maturer poems when involved in and surrounded by war, his style (and often his content) remained to a large extent impervious to its horrors. Certainly Douglas had none of Wilfred Owen's missionary zeal, and when he came to talk of war directly it was to the more intellectual Isaac Rosenberg that he turned:

> Living in a wide landscape are the flowers –
> Rosenberg I only repeat what you were saying –
> the shell and the hawk every hour
> are slaying men and jerboas . . .

In these lines the flowers and jerboas command attention as strikingly as the abstract shells and the men dying, though each is made the more actual by its association with the other. Douglas' great gift was his ability to bring a landscape to life with such a stroke and to make his poem contain its atmosphere – whether the Oxford of his student days or the cities and deserts of the Middle East where he was sent to fight. He didn't always write about war, and he did not need the war to discover his talent. Furthermore his experiences of a fast-moving tank warfare on various fronts were different in kind from those of the First World War poets in the trenches of Flanders.

The quality of simplicity is continually stressed by Douglas' admirers, and the lines of a poem he wrote in Oxford in 1940 are often cited: 'Remember me when I am dead/ and simplify me when I'm dead.' This same quality was dwelt on by Burns Singer in his poem 'In Memoriam: Keith Douglas':

> His was the grandest manner, assuming only
> One axiom of glory: simplify.
> He trusted God would teach him how to die
> And kept his language plain and homely.

But a true simplicity of style – one that is free from ornamentation and verbal excess, while at the same time able to contain the experience it confronts – is not arrived at easily. Ted Hughes stressed this in his Introduction to Keith Douglas' *Selected Poems*: 'It is not enough to say that the language is utterly simple, the musical inflection of it peculiarly honest and charming, the technique flawless. The language is also extremely forceful; or rather it reposes at a point it could only have reached, this very moment, by a feat of great strength.' The key is in that word 'moment', for it is the vibrant, actual moment – of a mood, an encounter, a landscape – which Douglas captures so engagingly. At Oxford these evocations are often tinged with nostalgia: an all-embracing war hovers in the background: carefree student days are ending:

> Well, I am thinking this may be my last
> summer, but cannot lose even a part
> of my pleasure in the old-fashioned art of
> idleness. I cannot stand aghast
> at whatever doom hovers in the background.

Here we see a young man living for the moment, intoxicated

1

The Chief General Manager
THE PRUDENTIAL ASSURANCE CO. LTD.
(Incorporated in England)
142, HOLBORN BARS
LONDON, EC1N 2NH

We love life

If you enjoy life now you'll still want to do so when you retire. And you'll need the money to enjoy it with

£10,000 when you retire
by taking out now a Prudential Endowment Assurance. For more details, complete and return this card.

Some examples
The value of Prudential policies has been amply demonstrated over the years, as is shown by these examples of payments on claims under Ordinary Branch with-profits endowment assurances for £5,000 taken out in the U.K., and which matured at age 65 on 1st January, 1971.

Age at entry	30	40	50
Sum assured	£ 5000	£ 5000	£5000
Bonuses*	£ 6325	£ 5065	£3360
Total payable	£11325	£10065	£8360

*Bonuses on future maturities cannot be guaranteed

Without committing myself in any way, I should like to have details of your Endowment Assurance policies.

Name

Address

Date of birth

Prudential
Assurance Company Limited

W & S (1444) 1112 CN 1/

by it and unwilling to cast it lightly aside. There is the sophistication of tone which was a hallmark of the other young Oxford Poets with whom Douglas was associated in the anthology *Eight Oxford Poets*, Sidney Keyes and John Heath-Stubbs among them.

It is indeed astonishing at how early an age Douglas found his own voice and direction, wriggling away quickly from Auden and Eliot. Perhaps his unsettled childhood was in part responsible. Born in Tunbridge Wells in January 1920, he was eight when his father left home, walking out of his life for ever. From then on he was under the sole charge of his mother. According to her, he quickly developed an independent and strongly individual character, anxious always not to be a burden. He went to boarding school, and in October 1939 to Oxford University, having won a scholarship to Merton. Already he was a voracious reader and a prolific writer, and at Merton was fortunate to have as his tutor Edmund Blunden, who encouraged him and helped to place his early poems. At Oxford, Douglas was in the centre of literary life: he edited *Cherwell* and an anthology of Oxford writing, *Augury*.

In the summer of 1941 he was sent to the Middle East. In his published journal *Alamein to Zem-Zem* he describes in brilliant detail the tank fighting at Alamein in which he was involved, and the ensuing offensive which drove the Germans from Africa. And in his poems of that period he managed to contain the whole essence of the desert – not only of war in the desert, but of the silence, immensity and mystery surrounding it. John Waller, who knew Douglas at Oxford and met him again in Cairo after the desert campaigns, remembers his mood at that time: 'He disapproved of what he considered to be the pseudo heroics exhibited by a number of war writers; his fundamental sense of realism prevented him from indulging in attitudes of this kind, and moreover he hated anything that could be called propaganda.'

In a letter from Egypt to his friend, the poet J. C. Hall,

Douglas expanded his views: 'I am surprised you should still expect me to produce musical verse. A lyric form and a lyric approach will do even less good than a journalistic approach to the subjects we have to discuss now. I don't know if you have come across the word Bullshit – it is an army word and signifies humbug and unnecessary detail. . . . To write of the themes that have been concerning me lately in lyric or abstract form would be immense bullshitting. . . . In my first poems I wrote lyrically, as an innocent, because I was an innocent: I have, not surprisingly, fallen from that particular grace since then. The change had begun during my second year at Oxford. . . . I am still changing. . . . My object (and I don't give a damn about my duty as a poet) is to write true and significant things in words which work for their keep. I suppose I reflect the absence of expectation – it is not quite the same thing as apathy – with which I view the world. As many others to whom I have spoken, not only civilians and British soldiers, but Germans and Italians, are in the same state of mind, it is a true reflection. I never tried to write about war . . . until I had experienced it. Now I will write of it, and perhaps one day cynic and lyric will meet and make me a balanced style.'

Nevertheless the images and motifs of the early work recur throughout his poetry. Stars, moons and ghosts are everywhere, but whereas those of Oxford were perhaps literary conceits, those of the Middle East were never so: in Oxford he wrote romantically of 'the speech of ghosts or leaves'; in Palestine, more realistically of meeting 'in dreams our own dishevelled ghosts'. In this way, gradually, experience began to inhabit the waiting crucible of his poetry. Towards the end of his short life (he was twenty-four when he died) it was quite clearly hardening his approach. He had a 'beast' on his back, a 'particular monster' which would not leave him or let him be; he saw men as 'trees suffering' and of his own life wrote poignantly:

And all my endeavours are unlucky explorers
come back, abandoning the expedition;
the specimens, the lilies of ambition
still spring in their climate, still unpicked;
but time, time is all I lacked
to find them, as the great collectors before me.

Those lines are from 'On a Return from Egypt', one of the last poems Douglas sent to Tambimuttu, the editor of *Poetry London*. Tambimuttu, who had included a number of Douglas' poems in his magazine and was preparing to publish them in book-form, recalls his first meeting with the young poet: 'After the occupation of Tunisia Keith visited me at the office and he already seemed to say the sentence he wrote in one of his letters, "I can't afford to wait because of military engagements which may be the end of me." He was in battle-dress; three cloth pips in yellow silk on a red background – I constantly caught myself out gazing at them – and the red beret of his Tank Regiment. I am reminded of the atmosphere of the room (for he changed it as soon as he entered) whenever I look at the two drawings he did for the dust jacket of his book of poems.'

When that posthumous book finally appeared in 1951 it was widely acclaimed. Reading it now one is immediately captivated by its freshness and linguistic verve. Its particular force and character are hard to define. The lines themselves of course are often haunting, musical though never lush. (Despite Douglas' views on lyricism, some of his most beautiful late poems are lyrical to the core: 'I Listen to the Desert Wind', for instance.) There is, too, something special in the sharpness of vision and the subtle shades it reflects; and in the poetic personality (witty, direct, oblique, lyrical, detached, by turn) which was able to take in the smoke and chat of a Cairo bar, the blues of a London dance hall, a colonel joking at the microphone, as easily as the bones of the dead themselves. Above all, he was thoroughly modern, his poems as much of the 70's as of the 40's he wrote in.

SIMPLIFY ME WHEN I'M DEAD

Remember me when I am dead
and simplify me when I'm dead.

As the processes of earth
strip off the colour and the skin:
take the brown hair and blue eye

and leave me simpler than at birth,
when hairless I came howling in
as the moon entered the cold sky.

Of my skeleton perhaps,
so stripped, a learned man will say
'He was of such a type and intelligence,' no more.

Thus when in a year collapse
particular memories, you may
deduce, from the long pain I bore

the opinions I held, who was my foe
and what I left, even my appearance
but incidents will be no guide.

Time's wrong-way telescope will show
a minute man ten years hence
and by distance simplified.

Through that lens see if I seem
substance or nothing: of the world
deserving mention or charitable oblivion,

not by momentary spleen
or love into decision hurled,
leisurely arrived at an opinion.

Remember me when I am dead
and simplify me when I'm dead.

TIME EATING

Ravenous Time has flowers for food
in Autumn, yet can cleverly make good
each petal: devours animals and men,
but for ten dead he can create ten.

If you inquire how secretly you've come
to mansize from the smallness of a stone
it will appear his effort made you rise
so gradually to your proper size.

But as he makes he eats; the very part
where he began, even the elusive heart,
Time's ruminative tongue will wash
and slow juice will masticate all flesh.

That volatile huge intestine holds
material and abstract in its folds:
thought and ambition melt and even the world
will alter, in that catholic belly curled.

But Time, who ate my love, you cannot make
such another; you who can remake
the lizard's tail and the bright snakeskin
cannot, cannot. That you gobbled in
too quick, and though you brought me from a boy
you can make no more of me, only destroy.

Wickwar, Clos., 1941

EGYPT

Aniseed has a sinful taste:
at your elbow a woman's voice
like, I imagine, the voice of ghosts,
demanding food. She has no grace

but, diseased and blind of an eye
and heavy with habitual dolour,
listlessly finds you and I
and the table are the same colour.

The music, the harsh talk, the fine
clash of the drinkseller's tray,
are the same to her, as her own whine;
she knows no variety.

And in fifteen years of living
found nothing different from death
but the difference of moving
and the nuisance of breath.

A disguise of ordure can't hide
her beauty, succumbing in a cloud
of disease, disease, apathy. My God,
the king of this country must be proud.

Egypt, 1942

I LISTEN TO THE DESERT WIND

I listen to the desert wind
that will not blow her from my mind;
the stars will not put down a hand,
the moon's ignorant of my wound

moving negligently across
by clouds and cruel tracts of space
as in my brain by nights and days
moves the reflection of her face.

Skims like a bird my sleepless eye
the sands who at this hour deny
the violent heat they have by day
as she denies her former way:

all the elements agree
with her, to have no sympathy
for my tactless misery
as wonderful and hard as she.

O turn in the dark bed again
and give to him what once was mine
and I'll turn as you turn
and kiss my swarthy mistress pain.

Wadi Natrun, 1942

WORDS

Words are my instruments but not my servants;
by the white pillar of a prince I lie in wait
for them. In what the hour or the minute invents,
in a web formally meshed or inchoate,
these fritillaries are come upon, trapped:
hot-coloured, or the cold scarabs a thousand years
old, found in cerements and unwrapped.
The catch and the ways of catching are diverse.
For instance this stooping man, the bones of whose face are
like the hollow birds' bones, is a trap for words.
And the pockmarked house bleached by the glare
whose insides war has dried out like gourds
attracts words. There are those who capture them
in hundreds, keep them prisoners in black
bottles, release them at exercise and clap them back.
But I keep words only a breath of time
turning in the lightest of cages – uncover
and let them go: sometimes they escape for ever.

El Ballah, 1943

VERGISSMEINICHT

Three weeks gone and the combatants gone,
returning over the nightmare ground
we found the place again, and found
the soldier sprawling in the sun.

The frowning barrel of his gun
overshadowing. As we came on
that day, he hit my tank with one
like the entry of a demon.

Look. Here in the gunpit spoil
the dishonoured picture of his girl
who has put: *Steffi. Vergissmeinicht*
in a copybook gothic script.

We see him almost with content
abased, and seeming to have paid
and mocked at by his own equipment
that's hard and good when he's decayed.

But she would weep to see today
how on his skin the swart flies move;
the dust upon the paper eye
and the burst stomach like a cave.

For here the lover and killer are mingled
who had one body and one heart.
And death who had the soldier singled
has done the lover mortal hurt.

Homs, Tripolitania, 1943

CAIRO JAG

Shall I get drunk or cut myself a piece of cake,
a pasty Syrian with a few words of English
or the Turk who says she is a princess – she dances
apparently by levitation? Or Marcelle, Parisienne
always preoccupied with her dull dead lover:
she has all the photographs and his letters
tied in a bundle and stamped *Décédé* in mauve ink.
All this takes place in a stink of jasmin.

But there are the streets dedicated to sleep
stenches and sour smells, the sour cries
do not disturb their application to slumber
all day, scattered on the pavements like rags
afflicted with fatalism and hashish. The women
offering their children brown-paper breasts
dry and twisted, elongated like the skull,
Holbein's signature. But this stained white town
is something in accordance with mundane conventions –
Marcelle drops her Gallic airs and tragedy
suddenly shrieks in Arabic about the fare
with the cabman, links herself so
with the somnambulists and legless beggars:
it is all one, all as you have heard.

But by a day's travelling you reach a new world
the vegetation is of iron
dead tanks, gun barrels split like celery
the metal brambles have no flowers or berries
and there are all sorts of manure, you can imagine
the dead themselves, their boots, clothes and possessions
clinging to the ground, a man with no head
has a packet of chocolate and a souvenir of Tripoli.

DESERT FLOWERS

Living in a wide landscape are the flowers –
Rosenberg I only repeat what you were saying –
the shell and the hawk every hour
are slaying men and jerboas, slaying

the mind: but the body can fill
the hungry flowers and the dogs who cry words
at nights, the most hostile things of all.
But that is not new. Each time the night discards

draperies on the eyes and leaves the mind awake
I look each side of the door of sleep
for the little coin it will take
to buy the secret I shall not keep.

I see men as trees suffering
or confound the detail and the horizon.
Lay the coin on my tongue and I will sing
of what the others never set eyes on.

Egypt, 1943

BÊTE NOIRE

(The trumpet swings out to blow you off the isle and dancers)

I

The trumpet man to take it away
blows a hot break in a beautiful way
ought to snap my fingers and tap my toes
but I sit at my table and nobody knows
I've got a beast on my back.

A mediaeval animal with a dog's face
Notre-Dame or Chartres is his proper place
but here he is in the Piccadilly
sneering at the hot musicians' skill. He
is the beast on my back.

Suppose we dance, suppose we run away
into the street, or the underground
he'd come with us. It's his day.
Don't kiss me. Don't put your arm round
and touch the beast on my back.

II

This is my particular monster, I know him;
he walks about inside me: I'm his house
and his landlord. He's my evacuee
taking a respite from hell in me
he decorates his room of course
to remind him of home. He often talks of going

Such a persuasive gentleman he is
I believe him, I go out quite sure
that I'll come back and find him gone
but does he go? Not him. No, he's a one
who likes his joke, he won't sit waiting for
me to come home, but comes

III

Yes, I too have a particular monster
a toad or a worm curled in the belly
stirring, eating at times I cannot foretell, he
is the thing I can admit only once to
anyone, never to those who have not their own.

Never to those who are happy, whose easy language
I speak well, though with a stranger's accent.

IV

If at times my eyes are lenses
through which the brain explores
constellations of feeling
my ears yielding like swinging doors
admit princes to the corridors
into the mind, do not envy me.
I have a beast on my back.

London, 1944

ON A RETURN FROM EGYPT

To stand here in the wings of Europe
disheartened, I have come away
from the sick land where in the sun lay
the gentle sloe-eyed murderers
of themselves, exquisites under a curse;
here to exercise my depleted fury.

For the heart is a coal, growing colder
when jewelled cerulean sea change
into grey rocks, grey water-fringe,
sea and sky altering like a cloth
till colour and sheen are gone both:
cold is an opiate of the soldier.

And all my endeavours are unlucky explorers
come back, abandoning the expedition;
the specimens, the lilies of ambition
still spring in their climate, still unpicked:
but time, time is all I lacked
to find them, as the great collectors before me.

The next month, then, is a window
and with a crash I'll split the glass.
Behind it stands one I must kiss,
person of love or death
a person or a wraith,
I fear what I shall find.

Egypt-England, 1943–44

SEAMUS HEANEY

SEAMUS HEANEY was born in County Derry, Ireland, in 1939. He is probably the best known of several gifted young Irish poets whose work has been commanding increasing attention over the past few years. His early pamphlet *Eleven Poems*, published in 1965 while he was at Queen's University, Belfast, already showed him to be an assured and attractive writer; and when his first book *Death of a Naturalist* was published a year later this early promise was confirmed. Apart from some neat metaphysical love lyrics, most of the poems in that volume (and indeed in its successor, *Door into the Dark*) are recreations of the farm he grew up on in County Derry, of the people who filled its landscape and circled its life. The countryside he writes of is possessed not only by man and beast but by myth and Irish history also. Thus he extends and complicates what is nowadays an over-worked genre, stamping it with his own personality.

'In these poems,' Heaney has said, 'I have tried to repossess in the act of concentration, in the act of writing, something of the fear and the fascination of those moments.' It is not just the accuracy of his descriptions which enables him to bring his 'farm' to life in the way he does, so that it becomes a microcosm of the conflicts and tensions of the human world outside; it is as much the fresh and vibrant quality of the language itself, and the sheer exhilaration with which the well-oiled verse forms speed it along. 'The power and precision of the poems are a delight', wrote Christopher Ricks in the *New Statesman*; while C. B. Cox exclaimed in *The*

Spectator: 'His words give us the soil-reek of Ireland, the violence of his childhood. ... The full-blooded energy of these poems make *Death of a Naturalist* the best first book of poems I've read for some time.'

Violence is certainly ever-present in the day-to-day life the poems evoke, but it has grown out of that life and not been willed on by the poet outside: hence it is of a different kind from that which animates the startling legendary creatures of Ted Hughes' recent verse. 'Purges' involving the drowning of cats or dogs are among 'the moments' Heaney had to come to terms with, together with more ominous supernatural ones as when (in the poem 'Death of a Naturalist') angry frogs invaded the flax-dam, turning the tables on the young frog-spawn-collecting boy:

> I sickened, turned, and ran. The great slime kings
> Were gathered there for vengeance and I knew
> That if I dipped my hand the spawn would clutch it.

Those 'slime kings' become more than mere frogs. The imaginative fire of the lines imbues them with some special phantasmagoric power. And although the fear is there, it is tinged with the fascination Heaney himself spoke of, a fascination and a rapport which the vibrancy of the language itself reveals. In 'An Advancement of Learning', another poem from that first book, the same fascination may be seen at work. Nobody *that* afraid would have stayed to observe with quite so curious an eye:

> Something slobbered curtly, close,
> Smudging the silence: a rat
> Slimed out of the water and
> My throat sickened so quickly that
>
> I turned down the path in cold sweat
> But God, another was nimbling

>   Up the far bank, tracing its wet
>   Arcs on the stones. Incredibly then
>
>   I established a dreaded
>   Bridgehead. I turned to stare . . .

In Heaney's work there is more than this recreation of the physical, which in any case is not confined to the animal world. He succeeds also in evoking the smell and feel of a particular place and the human involvement in it: the muscle, the creative energy, the almost sensual relish of the farmer at work – his grandfather:

>   Nicking and slicing neatly, heaving sods
>   Over his shoulder, going down and down
>   For the good turf. Digging.

Distanced now, writing years later from the city, the poet observes in conclusion:

>   Between my finger and my thumb
>   The squat pen rests.
>   I'll dig with it.

Heaney would maintain that this going backwards into the past was typical of Irish literature, and of Irish politics too – 'I suppose all Irishmen would say with Stephen Daedalus that history was a nightmare from which they were trying to awake.' This historical consciousness, this identification with the Irish character and the violent Irish present, is projected again and again in the poems, if always obliquely and in a context and through a landscape which is his authentic own. He has said of his poem 'At a Potato Digging', for instance, that he was using the potato field 'as an altar image, where the past is recalled and propitiated'. In this case it was of famine that he was thinking:

A people hungering from birth,
grubbing, like plants, in the bitch earth,
were grafted with a great sorrow.
Hope rotted like a marrow.

Stinking potatoes fouled the land,
pits turned pus into filthy mounds:
and where potato diggers are
you still smell the running sore.

The sense of drama and the enviable (Irish?) narrative skills
displayed in Heaney's first book are evident too throughout
its successor, *Door into the Dark* (1969), which was the 'Choice'
of the Poetry Book Society. To some extent his early subject
matter has remained – notably his preoccupation with crafts-
men and their skills (the thatcher, the blacksmith, the salmon-
fisher, the bull) and with the grievances of Irish history
('Requiem for the Croppies'). But while there are no startling
new directions, there are nevertheless new elements – a
growing fascination, for instance, with the sea, with its
symbolism and its echoes ('The Given Note'); and whereas
in an early love poem he could write, 'Never fear. We may
let the scaffolds fall/ Confident that we have built our wall,'
we now see (in 'Elegy for a Still-born Child') that wall
breached – the bleakness of the landscape he is driving through
poignantly reflecting his mood:

I drive by remote control on this bare road
Under a drizzling sky, a circling rook,

Past mountain fields, full to the brim with cloud,
White waves riding home on a wintry lough.

Cautiously praising *Door into the Dark* in the *New Statesman*
Anthony Thwaite wrote: 'It's impossible to fault the clean
language, sensuous delight, concise and modest statements;

and I'm sure it's all authentic. But I'm equally sure that the appeal of Heaney's work is of an exotic sort, to people who can't tell wheat from barley, or a gudgeon from a pike.' There may be some force in these remarks; but Heaney is a young and lively man with a sharp eye and a running mind, and one feels that he will yet have the last word. His latest poems already show an increasingly complex approach to more mysterious subjects. At present he is living and teaching at Berkeley, California. It remains to be seen what vigorous new landscapes enter his poetry.

Seamus Heaney writes:

A poet at work is involved in a double process of making and discovery, a process that at the best times is unique, unselfconscious and unpredictable. Every real poem that he makes represents a new encounter with what he knows in himself, and it survives as something at once shed and attained.

A poet begins involved with craft, with aspirations that are chiefly concerned with making. He needs a way of saying and there is a first language he can learn from the voices of other poets, dead and alive. To speak of this as apprenticeship is perhaps not completely accurate. It is a mimicry and a posturing that leads to a confidence, a voice of his own that he begins to hear, prompting behind lines he has learned.

Once the search to know the voice is over, the next problem is how to use it. Here craft passes into technique which is the ability to send the voice in pursuit of the self. Technique is dynamic, active, restless, an ever provisional stance of the imagination towards experience. It prospects for secrets and compounds resolutions. It divines and discovers the poet's meaning in and for the world.

I began to write poetry in 1963, craft-ridden, but compulsively attracted to those guardians of technique like the water diviner and the untutored musician, men whose wrists and fingers receive and uncode energies into meanings. To learn their ease and grace in the half-way station between the cellars of the self and the courtyards of the world around them has been and will be my study so long as I continue to write.

FOLLOWER

My father worked with a horse-plough,
His shoulders globed like a full sail strung
Between the shafts and the furrow.
The horses strained at his clicking tongue.

An expert. He would set the wing
And fit the bright steel-pointed sock.
The sod rolled over without breaking.
At the headrig, with a single pluck

Of reins, the sweating team turned round
And back into the land. His eye
Narrowed and angled at the ground,
Mapping the furrow exactly.

I stumbled in his hob-nailed wake,
Fell sometimes on the polished sod;
Sometimes he rode me on his back
Dipping and rising to his plod.

I wanted to grow up and plough,
To close one eye, stiffen my arm.
All I ever did was follow
In his broad shadow round the farm.

I was a nuisance, tripping, falling,
Yapping always. But today
It is my father who keeps stumbling
Behind me, and will not go away.

THE OUTLAW

Kelly's kept an unlicensed bull, well away
From the road: you risked fine but had to pay

The normal fee if cows were serviced there.
Once I dragged a nervous Friesian on a tether

Down a lane of alder, shaggy with catkin,
Down to the shed the bull was kept in.

I gave Old Kelly the clammy silver, though why
I could not guess. He grunted a curt 'Go by

Get up on that gate'. And from my lofty station
I watched the business-like conception.

The door, unbolted, whacked back against the wall.
The illegal sire fumbled from his stall

Unhurried as an old steam engine shunting.
He circled, snored and nosed. No hectic panting,

Just the unfussy ease of a good tradesman;
Then an awkward, unexpected jump, and

His knobbled forelegs straddling her flank,
He slammed life home, impassive as a tank,

Dropping off like a tipped-up load of sand.
'She'll do,' said Kelly and tapped his ash-plant

Across her hindquarters. 'If not, bring her back.'
I walked ahead of her, the rope now slack

While Kelly whooped and prodded his outlaw
Who, in his own time, resumed the dark, the straw.

THATCHER

Bespoke for weeks, he turned up some morning
Unexpectedly, his bicycle slung
With a light ladder and a bag of knives.
He eyed the old rigging, poked at the eaves,

Opened and handled sheaves of lashed wheat-straw.
Next, the bundled rods: hazel and willow
Were flicked for weight, twisted in case they'd snap.
It seemed he spent the morning warming up:

Then fixed the ladder, laid out well honed blades
And snipped at straw and sharpened ends of rods
That, bent in two, made a white-pronged staple
For pinning down his world, handful by handful.

Couchant for days on sods above the rafters
He shaved and flushed the butts, stitched all together
Into a sloped honeycomb, a stubble patch,
And left them gaping at his Midas touch.

REQUIEM FOR THE CROPPIES

The pockets of our great coats full of barley –
No kitchens on the run, no striking camp –
We moved quick and sudden in our own country.
The priest lay behind ditches with the tramp.
A people, hardly marching – on the hike –
We found new tactics happening each day:
We'd cut through reins and rider with the pike
And stampede cattle into infantry,
Then retreat through hedges where cavalry must be thrown.
Until, on Vinegar Hill, the fatal conclave.
Terraced thousands died, shaking scythes at cannon.
The hillside blushed, soaked in our broken wave.
They buried us without shroud or coffin
And in August the barley grew up out of the grave.

THE WIFE'S TALE

When I had spread it all on linen cloth
Under the hedge, I called them over.
The hum and gulp of the thresher ran down
And the big belt slewed to a standstill, straw
Hanging undelivered in the jaws.
There was such quiet that I heard their boots
Crunching the stubble twenty yards away.

He lay down and said 'Give these fellows theirs.
I'm in no hurry,' plucking grass in handfuls
And tossing it in the air. 'That looks well.'
(He nodded at my white cloth on the grass.)
'I declare a woman could lay out a field
Though boys like us have little call for cloths.'
He winked, then watched me as I poured a cup
And buttered the thick slices that he likes.
'It's threshing better than I thought, and mind
It's good clean seed. Away over there and look.'
Always this inspection has to be made
Even when I don't know what to look for.

But I ran my hand in the half-filled bags
Hooked to the slots. It was hard as shot,
Innumerable and cool. The bags gaped
Where the chutes ran back to the stilled drum
And forks were stuck at angles in the ground
As javelins might mark lost battlefields.
I moved between them back across the stubble.

They lay in the ring of their own crusts and dregs
Smoking and saying nothing. 'There's good yield,
Isn't there?' – as proud as if he were the land itself –
'Enough for crushing and for sowing both.'
And that was it. I'd come and he had shown me
So I belonged no further to the work.
I gathered cups and folded up the cloth
And went. But they still kept their ease
Spread out, unbuttoned, grateful, under the trees.

THE FORGE

All I know is a door into the dark.
Outside, old axles and iron hoops rusting;
Inside, the hammered anvil's short-pitched ring,
The unpredictable fantail of sparks
Or hiss when a new shoe toughens in water.
The anvil must be somewhere in the centre,
Horned as a unicorn, at one end square,
Set there immoveable: an altar
Where he expends himself in shape and music.
Sometimes, leather-aproned, hairs in his nose,
He leans out on the jamb, recalls a clatter
Of hoofs where traffic is flashing in rows;
Then grunts and goes in, with a slam and flick
To beat real iron out, to work the bellows.

ELEGY FOR A STILL-BORN CHILD

I

Your mother walks light as an empty creel
Unlearning the intimate nudge and pull

Your trussed-up weight of seed-flesh and bone-curd
Had insisted on. That evicted world

Contracts round its history, its scar.
Doomsday struck when your collapsed sphere

Extinguished itself in our atmosphere,
Your mother heavy with the lightness in her.

II

For six months you stayed cartographer
Charting my friend from husband towards father.

He guessed a globe behind your steady mound.
Then the pole fell, shooting star, into the ground.

III

On lonely journeys I think of it all,
Birth of death, exhumation for burial,

A wreath of small clothes, a memorial pram,
And parents reaching for a phantom limb.

I drive by remote control on this bare road
Under a drizzling sky, a circling rook,

Past mountain fields, full to the brim with cloud,
White waves riding home on a wintry lough.

THE GIVEN NOTE

On the most westerly Blasket
In a dry-stone hut
He got this air out of the night.

Strange noises were heard
By others who followed, bits of a tune
Coming in on loud weather

Though nothing like melody.
He blamed their fingers and ear
As unpractised, their fiddling easy

For he had gone alone into the island
And brought back the whole thing.
The house throbbed like his full violin.

So whether he calls it spirit music
Or not, I don't care. He took it
Out of wind off mid-Atlantic.

Still he maintains, from nowhere.
It comes off the bow gravely,
Rephrases itself into the air.

SHORE WOMAN

Man to the hills, woman to the shore. – Gaelic proverb

I have crossed the dunes with their whistling bent
Where dry loose sand was riddling round the air
And I'm walking the firm margin. White pocks
Of cockle, blanched roofs of clam and oyster
Hoard the moonlight, woven and unwoven
Off the bay. A pale sud at the far rocks
Comes and goes.
           Out there he put me through it.
Under boards the mackerel slapped to death
Yet still we took them in at every cast,
Stiff flails of cold convulsed with their first breath.
My line plumbed certainly the undertow,
Loaded against me once I went to draw
And flashed and fattened up towards the light.
He was all business in the stern. I called
'This is so easy that it's hardly right,'
But he unhooked and coped with frantic fish
Without speaking. Then suddenly it lulled,
We'd crossed where they were running, the line rose
Like a let-down and I was conscious
How far we'd drifted out beyond the head.
'Count them up at your end,' was all he said
Before I saw the porpoises' thick backs
Cartwheeling like the flywheels of the tide,
Soapy and shining. To have seen a hill
Splitting the water could not have numbed me more
Than the close irruption of that school,
Tight viscous muscle, hooped from tail to snout,

114

Each one revealed complete as it bowled out
And under.
            They will attack a boat.
I knew it and I asked John to put in
But he would not, declared it was a yarn
My people had been fooled by far too long
And he would prove it now and settle it.
Maybe he shrank when those thick slimy backs
Propelled towards us: I lay and screamed
Under splashed brine in an open rocking boat
Feeling each dunt and slither through the timber,
Sick at their huge pleasures in the water.

I sometimes walk this strand for thanksgiving
Or maybe it's to get away from him
Skittering his spit across the stove. Here
Is the taste of safety, the shelving sand
Harbours no worse than razor shell or crab –
Though my father recalls carcasses of whales
Collapsed and gasping, right up to the dunes.
But tonight such moving, sinewed dreams lie out
In darker fathoms far beyond the head.
Astray upon a debris of scrubbed shells
Between parched dunes and salivating wave,
I claim rights on this fallow avenue,
A membrane between moonlight and my shadow.

LIMBO

Fishermen at Ballyshannon
Netted an infant last night
Along with the salmon.
An illegitimate spawning,

A small one thrown back
To the waters. But I'm sure
As she stood in the shallows
Ducking him tenderly

Till the frozen knobs of her wrists
Were dead as the gravel,
He was a minnow with hooks
Tearing her open.

She waded in under
The sign of her cross.
He was hauled in with the fish.
Now limbo will be

A cold glitter of souls
Through some far briny zone.
Even Christ's palms, unhealed,
Smart and cannot fish there.

WILLIAM MEREDITH

WHEN William Meredith's third book of poems, *The Open Sea*, was published in 1958, Robert Lowell wrote: 'Meredith is an expert writer and knows how to make his meters and sentences accomplish hard labours. His intelligent poems, unlike most poems, have a character behind them.' More recently James Dickey spoke of him as 'a charming poet, cultivated, calm, quietly original, expansive and reflective, moving over wide areas slowly, lightly, mildly and often very memorably'. Such thoughtful compliments give some indication both of the respect William Meredith commands in his native America and of the nature of his reputation there.

Meredith, who is professor of English at Connecticut College, has himself lectured and written on a number of poets, Walt Whitman among them; but it was from Robert Frost rather than 'the careless genius' of Whitman that he took his early lessons – a debt he repays handsomely in a fine recent poem, 'In Memory of Robert Frost'. His first book of poems, *Love Letters from an Impossible Land*, was chosen by Archibald MacLeish in 1944 for the Yale Series of Younger Poets. Meredith, born in New York City in 1919, was then twenty-five: he had graduated from Princeton, served as a naval aviator in the war. Not surprisingly the poems' main theme was the war at sea. 'They stand,' wrote Richard Howard in *Athenaeum*, 'among the best poems of service in the Second World War, odes to duty that constitute a lamentable genre but a real distinction.'

Whatever the merits of those early poems – and style and

order are among them – they are not in any sense cataclysmic. The best catch quieter, personal moments, and it is only recently that Meredith has attempted to harness his highly-accomplished technical machinery to a directly public theme. Thus the poem 'A Mild-Spoken Citizen Finally Writes to the White House' (a recent one, included here) is something of a new departure; however, its intimate tone and careful structure ensure that concern rather than oratory is dominant. Its voice is that of a much-lived and cultivated man seeking direction in an age of 'swindling and killing'. The word 'finally' in the title is significant. In a recent interview Meredith declared: 'Only 25 years ago I was saying and hearing and believing that poetry was an end in itself. Poetry made nothing happen. Poetry now is supposed to make something happen. Some of it is going to be very bad, I expect, as propaganda poetry often is. But it is going to say things that are perfectly clear.'

The kinds of things Meredith has been saying in his poetry, clearly and perfectly, are not shouted from rooftops – or indeed sung from the stage, like the operatic arias he admires and which he defines in the poem 'About Opera':

> An image of articulateness is what it is:
> Isn't this how we've always longed to talk?
> Words as they fall are monotone and bloodless
> But they yearn to take the risk these noises take.

But while he may admire those risks taken in the spotlight, his own poems are clearly private affairs concerned above all with order: through them, one senses, *his* life finds order. In an introductory note to a Shelley Selection, Meredith wrote: 'Art by its very nature asserts two kinds of good – order and delight.' These two positive, if unfashionable qualities are characteristics of his own work. Whatever he celebrates, the language of the poem itself is part of that celebration. Generally it is relaxed and easy and where he has dedicated a poem to a particular person, as he has done often, he seems to be addressing that person directly. A need to communicate, to articulate a particular state of being can be sensed behind the actual lines, yet always the experience is ordered and asserted with a quiet sureness (and sometimes with a slyly engaging wit). The opening lines of 'For Guillaume Apollinaire' are an example:

> The day is colorless like Swiss characters in a novel
> And I sit at a desk in an old house left to the arts
> Teaching your poems English.

The direct, neutral tone takes the reader straight into the room of that old house to witness an act of communion between the two poets, a confrontation which is allowed to follow its own pace, reach its own unforced, perceptive conclusion:

> The house is a good place to work. And these poems –
> How quickly the strangeness would pass from things
>   if it were not for them.

It has been observed that behind the 'playful even chatty' tone of Meredith's verse is the movement of music. There is too a sense of scholarship, though the poems are in no way bookish. Nevertheless they are highly civilized, written by a man who has obviously absorbed his cultural heritage and whose roots go deep – a man who writes only of what he knows, as did Robert Frost, whom he 'captures' in an exact and affectionate elegy:

> Everyone had to know something, and what they said
> About that, the thing they'd learned by curious heart,
> They said well.
>   That was what he wanted to hear,
> Something you had done too exactly for words,
> Maybe, but too exactly to lie about either.

Everything here is dependent on the balance and tact of the lines, which carry the conversational tone beautifully. He 'knew' Frost, and it makes the poem a great deal more than a flat tribute: it has been willed into life and the form has followed. ('I wouldn't scan a poem while I was doing its important work – the first couple of drafts – any more than I would refer to a marriage manual at a critical moment: if the instinct fails, so will the act.')

The sea is one of various subjects Meredith has come to know at first hand, and it recurs as a theme throughout his work in a real and felt way. For instance, in the poem 'Carrier' (from his first book) the ship's easy movement is carefully matched by the rhythm and flow of the verse. The poet has identified completely with his subject and become part of it. The bombs and the flyers are there only in relation to the ship (the thing he knows). The poem is on a small canvas, but it does its job completely – as does a slightly later poem 'The Open Sea' with its evocative imagery and haunting music. In 'The Wreck of the Thresher', the title poem of Meredith's fourth book (1963), the approach is more ambitious. This elegy to the crew of a submarine lost at sea reflects (in the words of Daniel Hoffman) two of Meredith's abiding concerns, 'the threat of death and the loneliness of the sea . . . he deals with such themes pictorially, fixing his images as though in a painting, imposing upon them the designs imagination discovers and the forms and meters appropriated by a scrupulously sensitive ear.' The verse is perfectly attuned to its subject, the end and internal rhymes, the vocabulary itself and the atmosphere created by it, not only describing the sea but evoking it:

I stand on the ledge where rock runs into the river
As the night turns brackish with morning, and mourn
   the drowned.
Here the sea is diluted with river; I watch it slaver

Like a dog curing of rabies. Its ravening over,
Lickspittle ocean nuzzles the dry ground.
(But the dream that woke me was worse than the sea's
    grey
Slip-slap; there are no such sounds by day.)

More recently, in poems like 'Grievances', 'Effort at Speech',
and 'Winter Verse for His Sister', the hitherto tight verse forms
of Meredith's work have opened out, becoming more localized
and idiomatic – something that worries Meredith where British
readers are concerned: 'I worry about this because I don't think
I have given sufficient warning in every poem where I use a
low-keyed, personal American idiom. I use this native dialect
aggressively, not to say pig-headedly, but also I hope with
some subtlety, and this last may just do me in with an English
reader who generously credits me with speaking his own
tongue.'
    The subtlety is indeed there (compare the early 'Do not
Embrace Your Mind's New Negro Friend' with 'Effort at
Speech'), but the voice and vision, the areas and arias they
engage and uncover, are urgent enough to overcome such
barriers, drawing the reader into the world they shape.

William Meredith writes:

Lately I have been reading through the four books of verse –
perhaps 130 poems, mostly lyrics – that represent my entire
title to the name of poet. I have decided the reason they are
so few is not primarily laziness (although I agree with what
I think was Robert Frost's opinion that laziness, *of a certain
kind*, is a grace attractive to the Muse, just as busyness, of a
certain kind, strikes her as vulgar). Chiefly I think my

poverty of output stems from the conviction that an un-necessary poem is an offence to the art. What I would like to do in these remarks is clarify a little for myself and the reader what I mean by *unnecessary*.

The poem I am using as an example of the necessary is probably a rather disposable item of the 1940's. That is to say its integrity, as poem, may be provincial. But it *is*, or maybe only *was*, a necessary poem for me. Its subject – Civil Rights, I guess we would call it today – is a concern that my generation grew up with and have, on the whole, showed some responsi-bility about. But when this poem was written I was about 28 and my feeling about Negroes and Jews and other minorities was that of a young man much of whose adult life had been spent in military service and little of whose life had been spent familiarly with any except White Anglo-Saxon Protes-tants. At this point I should introduce the poem:

'DO NOT EMBRACE YOUR MIND'S NEW NEGRO FRIEND'

Do not embrace your mind's new Negro friend
Or embarrass the blackballed Jew with memberships:
There must be years of atonement first, and even then
You may still be the blundering raconteur
With the wrong story, and they may still be free.

If you are with them, if even mind is friend,
There will be plenty to do: give the liars lessons
Who have heard no rumors of truth for a long time
But have whatever they hear on good authority,
Whether it concerns Chinese women or the arts.

Expose the patrons, some of whose best friends
Are brothers, and who are never now anonymous:

What kind of credit do they expect for that,
Ask them, or better, ask their protested brothers,
The grateful tenants who can't get their curtsies right.

Finally the injured, who think they have no friend,
Who have been convinced by the repeated names
That they are Jews or Negroes or some dark thing:
They must be courted with the lover's touch
And as guiltily as if yourself had turned them inward.

If you complete this program, you will have friends
From all the rich races of your human blood:
Meantime, engage in the often friendless struggle.
A long war, a pygmy war in ways,
But island by island we must go across.

The poem suggests the beginning in me of a responsibility (I don't like to call it a guilt, because that word is so often used to suggest gloomy irresponsibility) about the most interesting and hopeful event of modern America. In the same volume with it, and I was almost 29 when it went to press, are some marvellously callow accounts of a less interesting America. But this poem seems to me *necessary* in the following terms. In it an aspiring poet, me, confronted something he did not understand: the inability of his culture to treat people with the respect and affection to which they were individually entitled. The Civil Rights movement has come a long way, and I blush a little at the innocence of the poem. But coming across it in the literature of the 40's I would not feel it was naïve historically. It is in fact a poem, feeling out a problem warily and with the powers of attention the poet could muster.

The files of *The Nation* for 1947 would be more interesting historically. In the same sense, the files of *The New York Times* during the Depression are more interesting historically than

Robert Frost's beautiful poem about bureaucracy called 'Departmental'. Poems have to be more sophisticated than history. Frost was not a politician, and I am not, even now, after three scary summers of teaching Negro high school kids, a Negro Leader. But when I wrote that poem, I had the kind of impulse that I feel the Muse approves. I was exploring, mostly for myself, a puzzle about which I had a glimmering. Maybe that is the likeliest prescription for a work of art: a puzzle about which one has a glimmering.

Now the difference between a poet's approach to his glimmering and that of a practical man is like the difference between art and propaganda. Art makes the error, in practical terms, of recognizing alternatives. It's a curious thing how certain angry works, works conceived in anger, like Goya's *Disasters of War* or *Madame Bovary*, are without propaganda value: *after such knowledge, what forgiveness?* they seem to say.

(My aunt, who comes from Alabama, is reported to have said on seeing the title of the poem, 'Well, I should hope not!' It is hard to read the poems of one's relatives as poems, but she was taking the matter too personally.)

The fact that it *is* a poem, of whatever quality, seems to the middle-aged man commenting on it now, demonstrable in a couple of ways. One is that the diction, by and large, is natural – something that cannot be said for half the poems in the volume with it. Another is that its form seems to grow fairly naturally out of its self-discovery. I have recently been teaching John Berryman's poem 'Winter Landscape', which seems to have fallen into five stanzas of five-foot verse with an elegance beyond my present skill, although Berryman wrote it at perhaps half my age. Nevertheless, my poem seems to me to have felt out a certain cinquefoil rhythm, and allowed that rhythm its trespasses. Like Richard Wilbur, whom I greatly admire, I have been accused of a sterile formality, and unlike Richard Wilbur, I have sometimes been guilty of it. This poem, and 2 or 3 poems a year ever since I was 21, suggest to me that when I pay attention, I find the form of the poem in the course of finding its content. The glimmering that an artist has is incarnate, if it is real. Form and content discover themselves simultaneously.

CARRIER

She troubles the waters, and they part and close
   Like a people tired of an old queen
Who has made too many progresses; and so she goes.
Leisurely swift her passage between green
   South islands; careful and helpless through the locks;
At lazy anchor huge and peacock vain.
On the streaked sea at dawn she stands to the streaks
   And when her way and the wind have made her long,
The planes rise heavy from her whining deck.
Then the bomb's luck, the guns' poise and chattering,
   The far-off dying, are her near affair;
With her sprung creatures become weak or strong
   She watches them down the sky and disappear,
Heart gone, sea-bound, committed all to air.

THE OPEN SEA

We say the sea is lonely; better say
Our selves are lonesome creatures whom the sea
Gives neither yes nor no for company.

Oh, there are people, all right, settled in the sea –
It is as populous as Maine today –
But no one who will give you the time of day.

A man who asks there of his family
Or a friend or teacher gets a cold reply
Or finds him dead against that vast majority.

Nor does it signify, that people who stay
Very long, bereaved or not, at the edge of the sea
Hear the drowned folk call: that is mere fancy,

They are speechless. And the famous noise of sea,
Which a poet has beautifully told us in our day,
Is hardly a sound to speak comfort to the lonely.

Although not yet a man given to prayer, I pray
For each creature lost since the start at sea,
And give thanks it was not I, nor yet one close to me.

THE WRECK OF THE THRESHER

(*Lost at sea, April 10, 1963*)

I stand on the ledge where rock runs into the river
As the night turns brackish with morning, and mourn the
    drowned.
Here the sea is diluted with river; I watch it slaver
Like a dog curing of rabies. Its ravening over,
Lickspittle ocean nuzzles the dry ground.
(But the dream that woke me was worse than the sea's grey
Slip-slap; there are no such sounds by day.)

This crushing of people is something we live with.
Daily, by unaccountable whim
Or caught up in some harebrained scheme of death,
Tangled in cars, dropped from the sky, in flame,
Men and women break the pledge of breath:
And now under water, gone all jetsam and small
In the pressure of oceans collected, a squad of brave men in a
    hull.
(Why can't our dreams be content with the terrible facts?
The only animal cursed with responsible sleep,
We trace disaster always to our own acts.
I met a monstrous self trapped in the black deep:
All these years, he smiled, *I've drilled at sea
For this crush of water*. Then he saved only me.)

We invest ships with life. Look at a harbor
At first light: with better grace than men
In their movements the vessels run to their labours
Working the fields that the tide has made green again;

Their beauty is womanly, they are named for ladies and
  queens,
Although by a wise superstition these are called
After fish, the finned boats, silent and submarine.
The crushing of any ship has always been held
In dread, like a house burned or a great tree felled.

I think of how sailors laugh, as if cold and wet
And dark and lost were their private, funny derision
And I can judge then what dark compression
Astonishes them now, their sunken faces set
Unsmiling, where the currents sluice to and fro
And without humour, somewhere northeast of here and
  below.

(*Sea-brothers, I lower to you the ingenuity of dreams,*
Strange lungs and bells to escape in; let me stay aboard last –
We amend our dreams in half-sleep. Then it seems
Easy to talk to the severe dead and explain the past.
Now they are saying, *Do not be ashamed to stay alive,*
You have dreamt nothing that we do not forgive.
And gentlier, *Study something deeper than yourselves,*
As, how the heart, when it turns diver, delves and saves.)

Whether we give assent to this or rage
Is a question of temperament and does not matter.
Some will have been done past our understanding,
Past our guilt surely, equal to our fears.
Dullards, we are set again to the cryptic blank page
Where the sea schools us with terrible water.
The noise of a boat breaking up and its men is in our ears.
The bottom here is too far down for our sounding;
The ocean was salt before we crawled to tears.

FOR GUILLAUME APOLLINAIRE

The day is colorless like Swiss characters in a novel
And I sit at a desk in an old house left to the arts
Teaching your poems English.
I have read the French words in the dictionary starting
                                                with 'W'.
They are borrowings, too: *wesleyen, wigwam, wisigoth*
And *wattman*, an archaic electrical-tram driver.
If you were alive this summer you'd be 82.

The fourth floor of the mansion, just less than an acre,
Is servants' country. For years it was settled –
Chambermaids, kitchenmaids, footmen, a butler, a cook.
Somewhere there must be almost an acre of them now
Laid out in the Romanesque floor plan under the sod,
And the lady who rang for them.
The house is a good place to work. But these poems –
How quickly the strangeness would pass from things
                                        if it were not for them.

ABOUT OPERA

It's not the tunes, although as I get older
Arias are what I hum and whistle.
It's not the plots – they continue to bewilder
In the tongue I speak and in several that I wrestle.

An image of articulateness is what it is:
Isn't this how we've always longed to talk?
Words as they fall are monotone and bloodless
But they yearn to take the risk these noises take.

What dancing is to the slightly spastic way
Most of us teeter through our bodily life
Are these measured cries to the clumsy things we say,
In the heart's duresses, on the heart's behalf.

FLEDGLINGS

FOR RUTH GAYLE CUNNINGHAM

*The twelfth grade at St. Joseph's High School
in Jackson, Mississippi*

As I talk to these children hovering on the verge
Of man and woman, I remember the hanging back
Of my own fledging, the alternate terror and joke
A child invokes, its claws frozen on the nest-edge.

Fly, I hear myself say now, though they're not my young,
And suddenly I see they are heavy as stones –
I see we are all of us heavy as stones –
How many years is it now I've been falling?

Then two of them, a thin, overbright white
Boy and a slower, steadier Negro girl,
Striking out, each make a fluttering whirl
And I know those two have already dreamt of the flight.

Oh, now the whole classroom is beating leaky wings
As if flying were a mere child's pantomime.
What a moment it is, what a mortal time –
Is there any plummet or flight as sheer as the fledgling's?

EFFORT AT SPEECH

FOR MURIEL RUKEYSER

Climbing the stairway gray with urban midnight,
Cheerful, venial, ruminating pleasure,
Darkness takes me, an arm around my throat and
      Give me your wallet.

Fearing cowardice more than other terrors,
Angry I wrestle with my unseen partner,
Caught in a ritual not of our own making,
      panting like spaniels.

Bold with adrenalin, mindless, shaking,
God damn it, no! I rasp at him behind me,
Wrenching the leather wallet from his grasp. It
      breaks like a wishbone,

So that departing (routed by my shouting,
Not by my strength or inadvertent courage)
Half of the papers lending me a name are
      gone with him nameless.

Only now turning, I see a tall boy running,
Fifteen, sixteen, dressed thinly for the weather.
Reaching the streetlight he turns a brown face briefly
      phrased like a question.

I like a questioner watch him turn the corner
Taking the answer with him, or his half of it.
Loneliness, not a sensible emotion,
      breathes hard on the stairway.

Walking homeward I fraternize with shadows,
Zig-zagging with them where they flee the streetlights,
Asking for trouble, asking for the message
                              trouble had sent me.

All fall down had been scribbled on the street in
Garbage and excrement: so much for the vision
Others taunt me with, my untimely humor,
                              so much for cheerfulness.

Next time don't wrangle, give the boy the money,
Call across chasms what the world you know is.
Luckless and lied to, how can a child master
                              human decorum?

Next time a switch-blade, somewhere he is thinking,
I should have killed him and took the lousy wallet.
Reading my cards he feels a surge of anger
                              blind as my shame.

Error from Babel mutters in the places,
Cities apart, where now we word our failures:
Hatred and guilt have left us without language
                              who might have held discourse.

IN MEMORY OF ROBERT FROST

Everyone had to know something, and what they said
About that, the thing they'd learned by curious heart,
They said well.
            That was what he wanted to hear,
Something you had done too exactly for words,
Maybe, but too exactly to lie about either.
Compared to such talk, most conversation
Is inadvertent, low-keyed lying.

If he walked in fear of anything, later on
(Except death, which he died with a healthy fear of)
It was that he would misspeak himself. Even his smile
He administered with some care, accurately.
You could not put words in his mouth
And when you quoted him in his presence
There was no chance that he would not contradict you.

Then there were apparent samenesses he would not
Be deceived by. The presidents of things,
Or teachers, braggarts, poets
Night offer themselves in stereotype
But he would insist on paying attention
Until you at least told him an interesting lie
(That was perhaps your field of special knowledge?)
The only reason to lie, he said, was for a purpose:
To get something you wanted that bad.

I told him a couple – to amuse him?
To get something I wanted? his attention?
More likely, respite from that blinding attention,

More likely, a friendship
I felt I could only get by stealing.
('All that I value was come by
By theft,' I wrote in a poem once. Explanation
Is a gift, like natural honesty.)

What little I'd learned about flying
Must have sweated my language lean. *I'd respect you
For that if for nothing else*, he said not smiling
The time I told him, thirty-two night landings
On a carrier, or thirty-two night catapult shots –
Whatever it was, true, something I knew.

WINTER VERSE FOR HIS SISTER

Moonlight washes the west side of the house
As clean as bone, it carpets like a lawn
The stubbled field tilting eastward
Where there is no sign yet of dawn.
The moon is an angel with a bright light sent
To surprise me once before I die
With the real aspect of things.
It holds the light steady and makes no comment.

Practicing for death I have lately gone
To that other house
Where our parents did most of their dying,
Embracing and not embracing their conditions.
Our father built bookcases and little by little stopped
    reading,
Our mother cooked proud meals for common mouths.
Kindly, they raised two children. We raked their leaves
And cut their grass, we ate and drank with them.
Reconciliation was our long work, not all of it joyful.

Now outside my own house at a cold hour
I watch the noncommittal angel lower
The steady lantern that's worn these clapboards thin
In a wash of moonlight, while men slept within,
Accepting and not accepting their conditions,
And the fingers of trees plied a deep carpet of decay
On the gravel web underneath the field,
And the field tilting always toward day.

GRIEVANCES

Now and perpetually, over
the dark side of the earth
flows a tide of wakefulness
through chosen men and women,
the changing hostels of grievance,
which travels by night.

In Dublin a huge old man
is falling to sleep, having for hours
rehearsed words for tomorrow
to say to his shiftless nephew,
his wife's son, who's been making
the flat upstairs a brothel

while a tossing girl in Rio
abruptly turns on the light
and getting out of bed
puts on a flannel bathrobe
and goes to the typewriter.
I have forgiven you for the last time . . .

This is the after-edge of night –
seen from far off, it's the last
dark segment before the purple band
that glows at the edge of the ball,
the edge of the planet that is
spinning again into sunlight.

Not thirty degrees east
the surly risers are throwing off

the fit, or trying to, faced with
idiot sun-cheer and bird-cheer,
the mindless smiles of dogs and children,
the accumulating evidence of day.

Meanwhile and perpetually, these
hoboes make a sour clock of our globe.
Choosing you once or often,
or settling in, they pass
through your town each night
and have to have lodging.

For the life of me, I can't
turn one away. In the morning
they write on the fence by your door
in cyphers no man can erase,
this one mails the letters
or, *this one says the words.*

A MILD-SPOKEN CITIZEN FINALLY
WRITES TO THE WHITE HOUSE

Please read this letter when you are alone.
Don't be afraid to listen to what may change you,
I am urging on you only what I myself have done.

In the first place, I respect the office, although one night
last spring, when you had committed (in my eyes)
criminal folly, and there was a toast to you, I wouldn't rise.

A man's mistakes (if I may lecture you), his worst acts,
aren't out of character, as he'd like to think,
are not put on him by power or stress or too much to drink,

but are simply a worse self he consents to be. Thus
there is no mistaking you. I marvel that there's
so much disrespect for a man just being himself, being his
    errors.

'I never met a worse man than myself,'
Thoreau said. When we're our best selves, we can all
afford to say that. Self-respect is best when marginal.

And when the office of the presidency will again
accommodate that remark, (Did you see? Fidel Castro
said almost that recently) it may be held by better men

than you or me. Meantime, I hear there is music in your
    house,
your women wear queens' wear, though winds howl outside,
and I say, that's all right, the man should have some ease,

140

but does anyone say to your face who you really are?
No, they say *Mr. President*, while any young person
feels free to call me *voter*, *believer*, even *causer*.

And if I were also a pray-er, a man given to praying,
(I'm often in fact careless about great things, like you)
and I wanted to pray for your office, as in fact I do,

the words that would come to me would more likely be
god change you than *god bless the presidency*,
I would pray, *God cause the President to change*.

As I myself have been changed, first my head, then my heart,
so that I no longer pretend that I don't swindle or kill
when there is swindling and killing on my nation's part.

Well. Go out into your upstairs hall tonight with this letter.
Generous ghosts must walk that house at night,
carrying draughts of the Republic like cold water

to a man parched after too much talk and wine and smoke.
Hear them. They are elected ghosts, though some will be
     radicals
and all may want to tell you things you will not like.

It will seem dark in the carpeted hall, despite the night-lights
in the dull sconces. Make the guard let you pass.
'If you are the President,' a shade with a water-glass

will ask you (and this is all I ask), calling you by name,
himself perhaps a famous name, 'If you are the President,
and things in the land have come to all this shame,

why don't you try doing something new? This building rose,
laborious as a dream, to house one character:
man trusting man anew. That's who each tenant is

– or an imposter, as some of us have been.'

Selected Bibliography

WILFRED OWEN:

    The Collected Poems of Wilfred Owen: Edited and Introduced by C. Day Lewis (Chatto & Windus).

    Wilfred Owen, Collected Letters: Edited by Harold Owen and John Bell (Oxford University Press).

    Journey from Obscurity - Memoirs of the Owen Family, by Harold Owen (Oxford University Press, 1963).

    The 1920 edition of Wilfred Owen's poems contains an Introduction by Siegfried Sassoon; the 1931 edition a Memoir by Edmund Blunden. Blunden's Memoir is included by Day Lewis as an Appendix to the edition of the *Collected Poems* listed above.

    Articles on the poets of World War I, and on Owen in particular, may be found in a special issue of the magazine *Stand* (Volume Four, No. 3), and an assessment of the Day Lewis edition of the *Collected Poems* in D. J. Enright's book *Conspirators and Poets* (Chatto & Windus, 1966).

PHILIP LARKIN:

    The North Ship (Fortune Press, 1945).

    The Less Deceived (Marvell Press, 1955).

    The Whitsun Weddings (Faber & Faber, 1964).

    Jill (Fiction: revised edition, including autobiographical introduction, Faber & Faber, 1964).

    An interview with Philip Larkin (by Ian Hamilton) appeared in *The London Magazine* of November 1964, and a statement by Larkin on his own work in the *Poetry Book Society Bulletin* (Autumn, 1964). Critical discussions of Larkin's work will be found in *Rule and Energy* by John Press (London, Oxford University Press, 1963); in *The New Poets* by M. L. Rosenthal

PHILIP LARKIN – *contd.*

(New York, Oxford University Press, 1967); in *The Modern Poet*, edited by Ian Hamilton (MacDonald, 1968); in *Contemporary Poets of the English Language* (St. James' Press, 1970).

THOMAS BLACKBURN:

The Next Word (Putnam, 1938).

A Smell of Burning (Putnam, 1961).

A Breathing Space (Putnam, 1964).

The Fourth Man (Macgibbon & Kee, 1971).

The Price of an Eye (Criticism: Longmans, Green, 1961).

A Clip of Steel (Autobiographical novel: MacGibbon & Kee, 1969; Panther Books, 1970).

A critique of Thomas Blackburn's work appears in *Rule and Energy* by John Press (London, Oxford University Press, 1963), and in *Contemporary Poets of the English Language* (St. James' Press, 1970). An interview with Thomas Blackburn is included in *The Poet Speaks* (Routledge, 1966).

KEITH DOUGLAS:

Collected Poems: Edited and Introduced by John Waller and G. S. Fraser (Editions Poetry London, 1951; Faber & Faber, 1966).

Selected Poems: Edited and Introduced by Ted Hughes (Faber & Faber, 1964).

Alamein to Zem-Zem (A Journal: Editions Poetry London, 1955; Faber & Faber, 1966).

A lengthy memorial article on Keith Douglas (by Tambimuttu) appeared shortly after his death in the magazine *Poetry London* (Vol. 2, No. 10), now available in the Cass reprint series of English Little Magazines.

SEAMUS HEANEY:

Death of a Naturalist (Faber & Faber, 1966).

Door into the Dark (Faber & Faber, 1969).

Articles on Seamus Heaney's work have appeared in the following magazines: by John Press in *The Southern Review* (Louisiana

SEAMUS HEANEY – *contd.*

University, U.S.A.), Summer, 1969; by Benedict Kiely in *Hollins Critic* (Hollins College, Virginia, U.S.A.), October 1970; and in the January 1971 issue of *Phoenix*.

WILLIAM MEREDITH:

The Open Sea and Other Poems (New York, Knopf, 1958).

The Wreck of the Thresher and Other Poems (New York, Knopf, 1964).

Earth Walk: New and Selected Poems (New York, Knopf, 1970).

Alcools, by Guillaume Apollinaire (Translator: New York, Doubleday, 1964).

Richard Howard includes a chapter on William Meredith's work in his critical book, *Alone With America* (London, Thames & Hudson, 1970), as does James Dicky in *Babel to Byzantium* (Farrar, Straus and Giroux, New York, 1968).